The Rhythm of Everyday Life

The Rhythm of Everyday Life

How Soviet and American Citizens Use Time

John P. Robinson, Vladimir G. Andreyenkov, and Vasily D. Patrushev

Westview Press
BOULDER, SAN FRANCISCO, & LONDON

A project of the U.S.–USSR Commission on the Humanities and Social Sciences of the American Council of Learned Societies and the Academy of Sciences of the USSR, administered in the United States by the International Research & Exchanges Board (IREX). Financial support for the American part of the research described in this report was provided by IREX, the Alfred P. Sloan Foundation, and the National Science Foundation; support was provided by the Academy of Sciences of the USSR for the Soviet part.

Published in 1989 in the United States of America by Westview Press, Inc., 5500 Central Avenue, Boulder, Colorado 80301, and in the United Kingdom by Westview Press, Inc., 13 Brunswick Centre, London WC1N 1AF, England

Library of Congress Cataloging-in-Publication Data
Robinson, John P.
    The rhythm of everyday life.
    Report of a study conducted under the auspices of
the Soviet Academy of Sciences and the Commission on
the Humanities and Social Sciences, American Council
of Learned Societies.
    Bibliography: p.
    Includes index.
    1. Time management surveys—Michigan—Jackson.
2. Time management surveys—Russian S.F.S.R.—Pskov.
3. Time management—Michigan—Jackson—Cross-cultural
studies. 4. Time management—Russian S.F.S.R.—Pskov—
Cross-cultural studies. 5. Quality of life—Michigan—
Jackson—Cross-cultural studies. 6. Quality of life—
Russian S.F.S.R.—Pskov—Cross-cultural studies.
I. Andreyenkov, V. G. II. Patrushev, V. D. (Vasilii
Dmitrievich) III. Title.
HN90.T5R64 1989   640'.43   88-5679
ISBN 0-8133-7576-2

Printed and bound in the United States of America

10   9   8   7   6   5   4   3   2   1

Contents

88-8313

Tables, Figures, and Maps

Foreword

This book describes an important advance in international social science research: the first jointly cooperative survey of representative samples of the United States and the Union of Soviet Socialist Republics. The study design was comprehensive, covering almost one thousand aspects of daily life in the two countries.

Although many people assume that cooperation between the two countries in a variety of fields has become possible as a result of recent improvements in Soviet-American relations, to a large extent the causal analysis should be reversed. As a result of work on the time-use project described in the pages that follow—work that proceeded even in the years of the poorest relations between the USA and the USSR—enormous experience was gained on what it takes to do a joint Soviet-American survey. This experience is now being put to use in a variety of comparative public opinion polls that would have been impossible otherwise.

Scholarly relations between the United States and the Soviet Union are now entering their fourth decade. Relations in the social sciences, most of which have been administered by the International Research & Exchanges Board, sponsored by the American Council of Learned Societies and the Social Science Research Council, quietly but extensively continued without interruption during the ups and downs of the overall relationship between the two countries. Indeed, the relations between the ACLS and the USSR Academy of Sciences are now the oldest set of uninterrupted relations between the USA and the USSR, with the exception of diplomatic relations themselves. Recognizing that Soviet-American scholarly relations needed to go beyond the exchange of individuals pursuing their own research, ACLS/IREX and the USSR Academy of Sciences established the Commission on the Humanities and Social Sciences in 1975 to sponsor collaborative research projects, symposia, joint publications, and the like.

From the first meeting of the Commission in March 1975 in Tarrytown, New York, sociology has been a major component of its work. At that meeting, Talcott Parsons, Eleanor Sheldon, Nikolai Mansurov, and other representatives of the discipline in the two countries recognized the desirability of moving as quickly as possible to perform and parallel joint survey research. Their sense was that work concerning social indicators was particularly relevant to the two countries and that among the indicators of mutual interest would clearly be the use of time. Subsequently, a meeting specifically on social indicators was held in Moscow in June

1976. After some additional administrative preparation and a conference on research in social indicators, in particular in the areas of time use and work, held at the Institute of Social Research in Ann Arbor, Michigan, in October 1979, the project got underway. Eventually, pilot studies were carried out in the Soviet Union and the United States in 1982–1983. After further work on the questionnaire, the study itself was carried out in the beginning of 1986. By that time, the researchers on both sides had participated in more than fifteen international meetings, each lasting from one to four weeks. They had also exchanged large amounts of written correspondence in the way of draft questionnaires, field organization plans and sample designs. If one adds to this the large volume of discussion by the national organizations of both countries representing the field as a whole, it is clear that much more than the ordinary effort had to be expended to achieve this landmark collaborative survey.

The topic of time use by the people of the two countries was selected for several reasons. First, time is a most useful and direct indicator of several revealing facets of daily life in the two countries, as can be seen in the findings of this volume. Second, it is a topic that researchers in both countries had studied jointly as part of the 1965–66 Multinational Time Use Project. Thirdly, precisely because there had been at least some contact in this field previously under international auspices, there was a sense that both sides would be comfortable with this area. Time use, therefore, constituted a good subject for a test case of whether or not the United States and the Soviet Union could work together to produce a joint survey.

An entire separate book could be written on the difficulties encountered along the way. Among them was the mistrust of many in the American sociological community of Soviet work with data and fears of possible Soviet tampering with data. This in turn drew indignation on the part of Soviet sociologists at what they considered both insulting and unjust. The Soviet scholars felt that this distrust created American demands concerning procedures that would not have been made of other countries. Despite this rocky beginning, arrangements concerning observation of data collection and access to data were eventually reached that proved satisfactory to all.

A second major problem was that of assuring funding for the surveys in each country, and this proved to be more of an issue for the American side than for the Soviet side. In general, it was considerably easier to reach agreement on the American side on the type of project desired than it was to obtain all the various approvals necessary on the Soviet side. Once the Soviet researchers had received the go-ahead for the project, things proceeded rather smoothly on the Soviet side. Implementation on the American side was more difficult in view of the need to assure funding for the project at an appropriate level once it was clear that it would be possible to proceed with Soviet colleagues.

Another problem that was eventually solved was communication between the two sides. In part, this was an issue of simply being able to obtain a response to a telex or letter fast enough, but in part it was also a question of translations from Russian into English and vice-versa and of ensuring the ability of researchers in both countries to work on their computers with the data sets.

Formally, there was never any break in the relations surrounding the project, and it is remarkable that the most important work went forward during the most troublesome period in Soviet-American relations. While changes in political relations did have some effect, it is fair to say that the structure and practices of the scholarly communities in both countries prevailed over the stormy climate of international relations.

It is a great pleasure to see the extensive data presented in this volume after many years of work that have gone into the project. Fuller causal analysis will surely follow, but it should be a great source of satisfaction to all concerned that it has been possible to provide such an extensive picture of the use of time in the United States and the Soviet Union.

Wesley A. Fisher
Secretary to the Commissions with the USSR
of the American Council of Learned Societies
International Research & Exchanges Board

Acknowledgments

This work would not have been possible without the help of many of our colleagues. They provided not only material support and professional expertise but also moral encouragement through long periods during which it seemed the project would never reach completion. It is because of their perseverance that this cross-national work exists, paving the way for more collaborative scientific research between our two countries in the future.

Paramount to the effort was the work of the International Research & Exchanges Board (IREX) on the American side and the USSR Academy of Sciences on the Soviet side. Both organizations provided the base support necessary to implement our long-range plans and meetings, both in the way of scheduling meetings and making technical arrangements and in writing protocols to coordinate our joint activity. On the American side, the untiring efforts and cultural expertise of Dr. Wesley Fisher are especially noteworthy.

Special appreciation on the American part of the project goes to the Alfred P. Sloan Foundation and to Dr. Michael Teitelbaum, who supported our work through that Foundation. Earlier support to complete the pilot phase of the project was provided by the National Science Foundation through the offices of Dr. Murray Aborn's section on Measurement Methods and Data Resources. Special thanks also go to Dr. Philip Stone of the Department of Social Relations at Harvard University, who provided technical and logistical expertise at crucial points of the project. Additional monetary and moral support was provided by Drs. Murray Polakoff and Stewart Edelstein of the Division of Behavioral and Social Sciences of the University of Maryland, College Park. We are also in the debt of Drs. Angus Campbell, Albert Reiss, and Eleanor Sheldon for their early general project negotiations, and to Drs. Thomas Juster and Philip Bosserman for their help and guidance in the pilot stage.

The implementation of the American part of the project would not have been possible without the skilled fieldwork of Sue Dowden, Norma Pecora, John Abrams, Tim Triplett, Jeff Holland, and Mike Wagner. Willard Cummings supervised the field data collection in Jackson with characteristic enthusiasm and efficiency—and minimal resources. Marilyn Roundy typed endless revisions of the manuscript, and Kim Remesch provided editing skills in final preparation—both of which are gratefully acknowledged.

On the Soviet side, major support was given by Dr. P. Fedoseev, the vice-president of the USSR Academy of Sciences, and Dr. G. Arbatov, co-chairman of the U.S.-USSR Commission on the Humanities and Social Sciences of the American Council of Learned Societies and the Academy of Sciences of the USSR. From the very beginning, time-use research between the two countries was promoted by Dr. T. Riabushkin, former director of the Institute for Sociological Research. The next director of the Institute (ISR), V. Ivanov, also provided long-term support, even during the most difficult periods of the project. Drs. T. Karachanova, M. Kosolapov, N. Lakomova, G. Tatarova, A. Chernikov, A. Kryshtanovskyh, and O. Voronkova actively helped as employees of the ISR in organizing the field phase of the project and in computer analysis of the data. Considerable help in translations between English and Russian as well as assistance on research organization was provided by Dr. V. Pogostin and S. Iampolsky. The mayor of Pskov and several municipal workers there also actively helped our researchers in the field stage of the project.

Last, but not least, a word of thanks to each of our respondents in Jackson and Pskov. They may have had little idea at the time about how essential their cooperation would be for the success of this project of international good will, but without their efforts we would have very little to say about the comparative ways of life in our two countries.

John P. Robinson
Vladimir G. Andreyenkov
Vasily D. Patrushev

1

Background

This volume presents the first results from a pioneering Soviet-American research project in the social sciences. A jointly administered methodology was developed for the project to examine both general and specific aspects of the use of time by the employed and non-employed populations in two cities: Pskov in the Soviet Union, and Jackson, Michigan, in the United States.

Our study identifies changes in the time-use patterns of both cities during the last two decades. In 1965, the same two cities were part of the Multinational Time-Budget Research Project, which included twelve socialist and capitalist countries. That project was the first social science venture in which capitalist and socialist countries took part (Szalai 1966). This new Soviet-American study built upon the experience gained in the earlier study and provided an ideal opportunity to see how several aspects of daily life had changed over the last two decades.

This study, however, moved well beyond simply documenting quantitatively how life had changed over the years. Indeed, it includes more than 600 other questions on descriptive aspects of daily life—how frequently did respondents engage in various activities beyond their single diary day, what levels of skills did respondents have to engage in various activities, what household technology did they have available, how did they feel about engaging in certain activities and what levels of satisfaction did they derive from these activities? The study went beyond the quantitative accounts of how much time was spent on activities to ask respondents various questions about the *meaning* of these activities in their daily lives.

The specific questions and hypotheses addressed are detailed later in this chapter and in Chapter 2. The study results are described in Chapters 3, 4, 5, and 6 and are summarized in Chapter 7.

Let us first turn to some general background description and conceptualization of the central study variable—time—for social science research. Time is one of society's most basic and most equitably distributed resources. Each of us has 168 hours each week, or 8,760 hours each year, to spend as we see fit. The activities we choose to engage in during that time reveal a great deal about our underlying motives, values and attitudes.

The variable of time also provides useful methodological properties for studying human behavior. It can be measured readily; moreover, it can be measured in basic units (minutes, hours, etc.) which are universally familiar. Societal life revolves around time schedules that both coordinate activities and order our daily lives. As Zerubavel (1981: p. 141) notes, "Time functions as one of the major dimensions of social organization along which involvement, commitment and accessibility are defined and regulated in modern society."

Time-based indicators are already familiar in social and economic accounts. Government and commercial agencies in different countries regularly collect and review data on the length of the workweek, hours of television viewed per day, time spent commuting to work, hospital-days of illness, and time spent on volunteer activities, among others. However, these official data are subject to several sources of distortion and ambiguity, as will be discussed shortly.

Time-use data can also function as an important zero-sum criterion for assessing processes of social change. If time spent on one activity increases (e.g., television), time spent on some other activity must decrease (e.g., radio, movies). As people move from one stage in the life cycle to another (e.g., parenthood, retirement), time-use data provide a direct measure of the impact of that change in behavioral terms. In much the same way, aggregate changes in how people spend time across historical periods can reveal fundamental changes in the character of daily life.

Time-use studies, therefore, provide expenditure data to test a wide variety of hypotheses about trade-offs and trends of daily life in society. Similar data are now being collected in more than twenty countries around the world to study trends in daily activities on several topics of long-range scholarly and policy interest—such as the informal economy, broadcast and print media usage, the "information society," the changing division of household labor, changing patterns of transportation and the increased diversity of leisure. While most of these issues can be addressed properly only with very large and intricately-designed time-diary studies, even modest time-diary data can indicate the plausibility of many of the contentions that are raised.

USSR Interests in Time Use Research

In Soviet research, time is conceived of as the medium through which the implementation of all human activity, both economically productive and non-productive, takes place. Time must be divided up to encompass the needs of a society as a whole and the needs of each family and its members. People's needs, and correspondingly the amount of time needed for satisfaction of those needs, change with the development of the society. Since the 168 hours available for use remains unchanged each week, changes that occur must occur within this structure.

The need for time is an objective, continual human phenomenon. That need conditions how time is converted into the various non-material forms of wealth in a society; how it is used by the people who live in that society. Sufficient time is needed for the satisfaction of daily, physiological, educational, and leisure needs, and for participation in public life. Like other forms of wealth, time is used and distributed by various classes and social groups for the satisfaction of their needs.

Social structure naturally places a significant stamp on how time is used. In the Soviet view, socialist society strives for an equitable distribution of time among classes and social groups to guarantee its rational use. It sees itself as a unique society in history, one that treats all time, both working and non-working, as the property of society as a whole.

Time is not only a form of wealth, but a measure of activity as well. While Soviet sociologists realize that Karl Marx considered working time as a measure of labor, various forms of non-working time are, to the same extent, measures of other forms of human life activity. As a measure of activity, time essentially acts as an index of its effectiveness. Thus, the expenditure of working time is an objective index of the effectiveness of labor and serves to define its productivity. In the same way, the time the population spends shopping becomes an index of the effectiveness of a society's trade network or marketing system. The control by society of proper distribution and use of time by various social groups in the population has become an important social concern. This task is especially urgent in the USSR's current period of accelerating socio-economic development.

It is important to remember that the first study of the use of time by various social groups in the world was the one undertaken in the USSR in the 1920s. During the 1920s and 1930s, and then in the 1950s and 1960s, significant research experience was gained on how to conduct such studies. Time budgets of various social groups were studied and certain ways for improving time use became understood. By the beginning of the 1960s, a number of other socialist countries (Bulgaria, Hungary, etc.) had also begun to undertake time-budget studies.

However, these were still local studies. Although enormous bodies of factual data were amassed, they were collected by different techniques, at different periods in time and with different scientific or policy goals. That made comparison of data most difficult. There arose an obvious need to conduct a cross-national comparative study of time budgets. Under the leadership of the Hungarian sociologist Alexander Szalai (1972), a joint 1965–66 multinational study was conducted of urban communities in twelve socialist and capitalist countries, including the Union of Soviet

Socialist Republics and the United States. Data collections and coding methods developed largely on the basis of the Soviet research experience in conducting time-budget studies were employed in the project.

Three basic aims were envisaged in this earlier program of cross-national research:

- the measurement of the distribution of types of daily activity and the influence of industrialization and urbanization on these ways of life in the urban population;
- the development and testing of a technique of comparative international study of time budgets of the urban population, applicable for various countries; and,
- the promotion of expanded international collaboration in the study of time use.

In the USSR, the city of Pskov was chosen as the target community. This was done in accordance with the following criteria established by the multinational project:

1. It should be a small, independent industrial city (not a suburb), with at least 30 percent of its able-bodied population employed in local industries. Various branches of the economy should be represented, with not more than 25 percent of the workforce involved in the agricultural sector, and not more than 5 percent who work outside the territory of the city.
2. The city's population should range between 30,000 to 280,000 people.
3. The boundaries of the city should also include suburban settlements, whereby about 5 percent of these suburbanites commuted to work in the city.[1]

The first time-budget survey of the Pskov population was conducted in October and November of 1965. As part of an international research project Soviet sociologists discovered both regularities and peculiarities in the use of time by Pskov residents in comparison to the urban populations of various other countries. The data also suggested various influences and processes of industrialization and urbanization. These conclusions and results of the 1965–66 data are reflected in many publications.[2]

Several socio-economic processes have affected life in the USSR since 1965. There has been further industrial development, an increase in the population of cities, continued growth in the education and well-being of the population, and new developments in consumer services. These have naturally resulted in certain changes in people's way of life and use of time. The need to describe the changes that had occurred became important to (a) understand the regularities and trends in the ways of life of the urban population, and (b) adopt administrative decisions for improving the socialist way of life.

Patterns of change in the population's use of time have long attracted the attention of sociologists. There are a number of publications devoted to sufficiently comparable groups of the population or for sufficiently long spans of time.[3] However, there are very few cities in the USSR for which time-budget data for the entire adult population (from age 18 upward) have been collected. Besides Pskov, the cities that have been studied before 1986 included Rubtskovsk, Kerch and a few small cities in Lithuania and Latvia.

The best opportunity for studying trend data on changes in the way of life of the urban USSR population, then, comes from Pskov. This small city is typical of the European part of the country, with its highly developed industry, consumer and cultural services. Since 20 years have passed since the first study, there has been sufficient time for the changes in the life of society to be reflected in the population's use of time.

Thus the concrete tasks of the current research project in Pskov were formulated as follows:

- Measure the current duration, frequency, place of occurrence and social setting of the daily types of activity;
- Indicate the influence of processes of industrialization and urbanization on the way of life of this urban population;
- Identify patterns of change in the duration and structure of daily types of activity of various groups of the urban population;
- Analyze the opinions and social attitudes of the urban population regarding the use of working time, time for household and leisure activities, the satisfaction with the various dimensions of time and conditions for its use, value orientations toward time, etc.; and,
- Improve general techniques for the study of the use of time.

U.S. Interests in Time Use Research

Perhaps the main interest in U.S. studies of the use of time is on social change. Earlier longitudinal studies of time-use changes in the United States have shown how several daily activities have changed over the last half century. More focused subsequent studies analyzed the results of the introduction of the television into society, how American reading habits have changed and how the sexual division of household labor has shifted across the decades.

Before the 1986 study described in this report, four national level time-diary studies had been conducted. These four studies and the organizations involved are as follows:

1. *Mutual Broadcasting Corporation* (1954) study, in which more than 8,000 American adults aged 15–59 kept time diaries for a two-day period.
2. *Survey Research Center, University of Michigan* (1965) study, in which 1,244 adult respondents aged 18–64 kept a single-day diary of activities, mainly in the fall of that year; respondents living in rural areas, and non-employed households were excluded. The 1966 Jackson study was designed as one-half of the U.S. participation in the multination study.
3. *Survey Research Center, University of Michigan* (1975) study, in which 1,519 adult respondents aged 18 and over kept diaries for a single day in the fall of that year; in addition, diaries were obtained from 788 spouses of these designated respondents. This sample was fully national, including rural and non-employed households and those aged 65 and older.
4. *Survey Research Center, University of Maryland* (1985) study, in which 4,958 respondents aged 18 and older kept or reported diaries for a single day. Unlike earlier studies, this fully national study was conducted across the entire calendar year of 1985, and employed three modes of data collection: mailback, telephone and personal.

The 1986 study described in this present report was designed specifically to be compatible with the 1965 (and 1975/1985) studies and thus to continue these earlier efforts to measure trends in time use across the last twenty years.

In addition to these national-level studies, several significant community-level studies have been conducted with differing emphasis on the interests of the sociologists who contributed to the studies. These include the many studies of women's time (particularly farm housewives) conducted in the 1920s and 1930s (as summarized in Vanek 1974), the pioneering sociological studies of Westchester County in New York State by Lundberg et al. (1934) and of Boston young adults by Sorokin and Berger (1939), the study of rural-urban lifestyle differences by Reiss (1959), the studies of homemakers' use of time in New York State by Walker (1969), and the important work of combining temporal and spatial variables by Chapin (1974). As noted below, the results of these studies generally produced results that were consistent with those in the national studies.

The Measurement of Time Use

The most familiar time accounts in American society have been gener-
ated from simple estimates of time expenditures given by respondents to
survey interviewers. Such estimates are subject to several problems. While
respondents may be able to give reliable estimates of the time they spend
on certain activities (particularly if they are done on a regular or paid
basis, such as work-related activities), the respondent estimate approach
is subject to several sources of distortion: ambiguities of activity and time
boundaries, respondent self-perception and self-projection, social desirability, memory and recall difficulties, and handling of atypical days or
weeks, among others. Moreover, in general, it seems unreasonable to
expect respondents to give accurate off-the-cuff estimates of the time they
spend in diverse activities, such as doing housework or engaging in leisure, or even in specific activities such as watching television or reading.

The value of the one-day, time-diary approach is that it overcomes these
limitations by focusing on a clearly defined time period that involves
minimal memory loss, particularly if respondents are asked to report their
activities for the preceding day (i.e. "yesterday,") or are asked to keep the
diary for the following day (i.e. the "tomorrow" approach). The 24-hour
duration is also a period that is convenient, familiar, and manageable for
respondents to reconstruct, and it automatically covers and represents all
daily activities. The resulting difficulty, however, is that the particular day
chosen is a very short period from which to generalize about the overall
behavior of that individual. But when aggregated, time diaries provide a
very rich, reliable, and complete source of data on groups of individuals
for almost all forms of daily activity.

Thus, there is widespread interest in time-diary data on time spent at
the workplace, travel time, housework (both on basic household chores
and for more expressive tasks such as cooking and decorating), time
"invested" in child care, time spent shopping, time spent eating at the
house or away from home, time spent being involved in educational
activities or organizational participation, social visiting and interaction,
cultural activity (arts performances, movies, sports events, etc.) outside
the home, recreational pursuits and hobbies, conversation, resting-relax-
ing and mass media usage.

The value of time-diary data is particularly evident with regard to mass
media activity in America. Time-diary data provide a unique perspective
on the larger role of these media, particularly as the various media relate
to each other and to the amount of free time available. Few time estimates
available from television rating or commercial media sources, for example,
contain data on multiple media use on a daily basis or relate media use to
available free time. As a result, many estimates from commercial media

sources about television time exceed estimates of free time that respondents report in their time diaries. Reasons for greater confidence in the data from time diaries are discussed below.

Methodological Options in Time-Use Measurement

Time diaries can provide national estimates of a wealth of time expenditure variables of academic and policy research interest. It is for the above-mentioned reasons that there has been such an upsurge of time-diary studies in other countries and an expanded international network of researchers interested in time-use studies. Researchers in more than twenty countries have conducted time-diary studies with representative samples of their population over the last twenty years.

These various studies have used the myriad options available to researchers collecting or reporting daily activity patterns in these various countries. These methodological variations for the survey interview method of diary reporting include:

- Conducting interviews by telephone, by mail or in person;
- Having the data collected by academic, governmental or commercial research agencies;
- Specifying the purposes of the data collection (e.g., for media use or for household work) vs. providing no cues about the purpose of the survey or the organization(s) that sponsored the study or that would use the study results;
- Having the data collected across the year vs. certain months/seasons of the year;
- Having the data collected to include weekends as well as weekdays, or to include holiday/vacation days as well as "normal" periods of the year;
- Having respondents report on one day's activities vs. having them report for several days (including recall for one specified day several days after that day);
- Including the full 24 hours of the day vs. only shorter periods of the day (e.g., 5–11 p.m., usual working hours, some "random hour" or two-hour periods);
- Identifying specific categories of time (e.g., 10–10:15 a.m.) vs. leaving the time periods open; that is, dependent on the length of activities reported by respondents;
- Assigning activities into pre-coded "closed" categories vs. having respondents/observers report activities in an open-ended format using their own words and frames-of-reference;
- "Framing" the activity report (e.g., by first having respondents report

periods of time away from home, or in transit) vs. reporting on a simple, serial basis throughout the day; and,

- Including ancillary diary questions on "secondary" activities, location of activities, or presence of social partners in the activity.

Despite these sources of methodological variation across organizations around the world in using all of these various options in their data collections, the present literature provides little empirical support that would hold any one of these methodologies as superior to the other.

Almost all studies, however, depend on the self-report method rather than on some form of observation. That is an unfortunate situation since it leaves these self-report data open to basic questions of validity, in the sense of being verifiable by some independent method of observation or report. But there are encouraging signs from the few and limited observational studies that have been done (Juster 1985; Robinson 1977; Bechtel et al. 1972; Allen 1968). There are also several studies that have established the aggregate reliability of time-diary data (e.g., Robinson 1977; Szalai et al. 1972), even across studies using different diary formats (e.g., Chapin 1974; Walker 1969). Thus, aggregate results from the 1965–66 Jackson study correlated .88 with those from the 1965 national study.

In the present study, then, we used essentially the same diary procedures as in the 1965–66 study. This was a time diary in which individuals reported all their daily activities. One sample page from this form is illustrated in Table 1.1. It can be seen that this form is completely open-ended, requiring respondents to report not only all their primary activities across the day, but also the starting and ending times for each activity, its location, the presence of other people, and the secondary activities that accompany each primary activity.

The main differences in the 1986 study included the use of a more elaborate activity-coding scheme, and interviewers spent less time interviewing respondents in the "warm-up" first contact with respondents. Respondents were also asked to complete a 36-page questionnaire in addition to the leave-behind diary; no such questionnaire was left behind in the 1966 study, and that made the 1986 interviewers' job a more challenging one.

History and Evolution of the Project

The Soviet-American project, "The Use of Time and Its Indicators," was developed within the framework of the U.S.-USSR Commission on the Humanities and Social Sciences of the American Council of Learned Societies and the Academy of Sciences of the USSR. Begun on the initiative of the International Research & Exchanges Board in 1975, the

Table 1.1
Sample Diary Page

Time	What Did You Do?	Time Began	Time Ended	Where?	List Other People With You	Doing Anything Else?
				What You Did from Midnight Until 9 in the Morning		
Midn						
⇒						
1 AM						
⇒						
2 AM						
⇒						
3 AM						
⇒						
4 AM						
⇒						
5 AM						
⇒						
6 AM						
⇒						
7 AM						
⇒						
8 AM						
⇒						

Commission was established to broaden the types of contact between Soviet and American scholars beyond the exchange of individuals pursuing their own research. Representatives of the field of sociology from both countries reached consensus at the first meeting of the Commission, held in the USA in 1975, that research on social indicators was an area of clear mutual interest and that cooperation on surveys was a goal to be pursued. Subsequent discussions evolved in agreement that a project on time use be supported.

Four large stages in the evolution of the project can be distinguished in the chronology outlined in Table 1.2. In the first stage, certain general topics for study were chosen, the ideas of the project were specified by official agreements and the two research teams were formed. This stage occurred approximately during the period from 1976 to 1979, and concluded with the first conference of Soviet and American sociologists in Ann Arbor, Michigan, in October, 1979.

The second stage involved identifying the themes of the research project and their instrumentation. This stage began with a meeting of the project's working groups in Moscow during March and August of 1981. These meetings produced an informal agreement about the goals of the project, a first draft of the questionnaire and a classification of types of activity to be examined. The completed documents were reviewed and elaborated upon during a working meeting in the U.S. in October–November 1981 with Andreyenkov and Patrushev on the Soviet side, and Robinson and Dr. Thomas Juster on the American side. The preparation of the draft questionnaire for acquiring survey data about inserting subjective opinions regarding the uses of time involved the longest and most difficult discussion, and several sources of cross-national difficulties and disagreements over appropriate question framing and survey methodology had to be overcome. These arose not only because of substantial differences in the ways of life of the population of the two countries, but also because of the different field experiences of the researchers in the U.S. and the USSR. Matters related to the study of time budgets were more simple, since earlier agreement had been reached to replicate the techniques used in the 1965–66 international comparative study.

The project's third stage in 1982–83 involved completion of the instrumentation and conduction of pilot studies in both countries. In the USSR, the pilot study was conducted in two stages in Kerch, a city with a population of 168,000 situated in Crimea near the Black Sea. The first stage was in the spring of 1982 with a time-diary survey of 698 residents, and the second stage occurred in the spring of 1983 with a re-interview of 655 of these respondents concerning their opinions about how their time was used. In the United States, parallel time-diary and opinion data were collected in the spring of 1983 in three Maryland cities: Hagerstown,

Table 1.2
Chronology of the Soviet-American Time Use Project

Date	Place	Activity
1976 (June)	USSR	Meeting of the official U.S.-USSR representatives in sociology. Formulation of themes for collaborative research on social indicators.
1977 (June)	USSR	Second meeting of the U.S.-USSR Commission on the Humanities and Social Sciences. Joint decision to exchange analytical surveys on time use themes, among others, and to discuss them at future conferences.
1978 (February)	USSR	Administrative meeting of official representatives to discuss preparations for a joint conference in the U.S.
1979 (October)	U.S.	Conference of official representatives and of American sociologists interested in the project. Further discussion of potential survey topics and elaborations of the general framework for joint projects, and the choice of partners in the U.S. and the USSR.
1981 (March)	USSR	First meeting of the project's working groups. Identification of the major themes and purposes of the project, and of the plans needed to implement and complete the project.
(August)	USSR	Second meeting of the working groups. Discussion of the first draft version of the questionnaire and diary forms.
(October-November)	U.S.	Third meeting of groups to develop specific plans of research, prepare a final draft of the survey instruments, and search for financial support for the American side for the project.
1982 (April-May)	USSR	Conduct of pilot study of time budgets in the USSR city of Kerch (698 respondents).

Table 1.2—continued

Date	Place	Activity
1982 (October)	USSR	Fourth meeting of working groups. Discussion of the basic directions and themes of the comparative analysis of data. Formulation of criteria for the choice of major topics for comparison within a larger plan of comparative research. Discussion of American side's continued search for financial support.
1983 (March)	USSR	Fifth meeting of the working groups. The American side receives financial support from the National Science Foundation. Working groups agree on the final version of the questionnaire for the pilot study.
(Spring)	USSR/ U.S.	Pilot questionnaire studies of the opinions of residents about the use of time in Kerch (in the USSR) and three Maryland cities (in the U.S.).
1985 (May)	U.S.	Sixth meeting of the working groups. Discussion of the first results of the pilot study questionnaire, and implications for refining methodological procedures. Joint visit to the American research site, the city of Jackson.
(July)	USSR	Seventh meeting of the working groups for the discussion of the results of the pilot survey of time budgets and refinement of the field procedures. Joint visit to the Soviet research site, the city of Pskov.
(November)	USSR	Eighth meeting of the working groups. Discussion of final data coding and analysis plans and exchange of back-translated questionnaires. Final financial support from the Sloan Foundation for the American data collection.
1986 (January-February)	USSR	Data collection in Pskov. Ninth meeting of working groups. Americans observe field procedures in Pskov and finalize ways to make U.S. data collection as comparable as possible.

Table 1.2—continued

Date	Place	Activity
1986 (February-May)	U.S.	Data collection completed in Jackson.
(Spring-Summer)	USSR/ U.S.	Computer input of data, editing the data, preliminary tabulations of the data, and preparing tables for exchange.
(September)	USSR	Tenth meeting of working groups. Examination of preliminary tabulations from both countries. Plans for outlining project monograph and for multivariate data analyses.
1987 (February)	USSR	Eleventh meeting of working groups. Exchange of initial data frequency distribution and cross-tabulations. Preparation of a short report on the results of the research. Outline of contributions for monograph describing study results.
(July)	USSR	Twelfth meeting of working group. Exchange of draft chapters of project monograph. Presentation of results to joint symposium from the American Sociological Association and Soviet Sociological Association in Vilnius.
(September)	U.S.	Thirteenth meeting of working group. Revision of chapters for monograph. Exchanges of additional analysis tables.

Cumberland and Salisbury. In this pilot study, 412 respondents completed a time diary and questionnaire at the same time.

The project's fourth and final stage was concerned with the carrying out of the main survey. Based on the pilot study experiences and review, questionnaire and diary procedures were revised and "back translated" from Russian to English. The basic survey in the USSR was conducted in Pskov in January and February of 1986, and in the United States in Jackson mainly in February and March of 1986.

Concerns and Questions of the Present Study

The 1986 studies in Pskov and Jackson, then, allowed researchers an opportunity to examine several issues of mutual interest. Most directly, it provided an opportunity to observe how several quantitative features of daily life had changed over the previous two decades. In which ways had daily activity patterns become more similar, probably reflecting larger global shifts in advanced industrial societies due to the influence of changing, or increased availability of, technology in the two countries? Conversely, in which ways had daily life become more different, mainly reflecting the character of life in each country due to its unique sociopolitical or cultural forms of organization?

More specifically, results from the 1965–66 study (Szalai et al. 1972) had suggested that television had played a central role in virtually revolutionizing free-time activities in countries in which it had been introduced. While television had reached more than 95 percent of the American households in 1965, it had reached far fewer homes in the Soviet Union; for example, less than half (49 percent) of the 1965 respondents in Pskov reported they had access to a television set in their household. As the proportion of households with television grew, would one find the same kinds of activity displacement that had occurred in other Western and Eastern countries, particularly in the decreased use of other mass media such as radio listening, cinema attendance and reading? In which groups of society would these effects be most clearly seen—among men or women, among married or non-married, among older or younger, or among better educated or less educated?

In much the same way as the technology and sophistication of television has developed, there have been great advances in the availability of household technology in both countries designed to reduce the burdens of household work. This technology makes it possible for women to reduce the time they spend doing household work. This can function both directly and indirectly—by allowing men increased opportunity to participate in these activities, for example. Moreover, at the same time, there was further pressure to reduce time on housework due to various women's movements that had raised questions and consciousness about the implicit value and status of such activities. Such reductions in time on housework would help reduce the "dual burdens" on working women which had been recognized formally as a central social policy issue in the USSR, and highlighted in women's movements toward gender equality in the United States.

In addition, there have been the continual pressures to reduce time spent at the workplace in both countries. One of the hallmarks of a technologically-advanced society in the 20th century has been the ability to reduce paid work time and increase the free time of the population. Decreased ages of retirement and increased years of formal education have much the same effect in increasing free time across a person's lifetime. How much are these changes reflected in work time reported in time diaries?

At the same time, the 1965 study revealed several unique ways of spending time in the two countries. Time spent waiting in line or queues, for example, was particularly high in the Soviet Union. Soviet respondents were also significantly more likely to report time spent reading books than were respondents in other countries, suggesting that Soviets could be more resistant to change as a result of television. Soviet citizens also spent more time attending educational courses and lectures, and conversely, they also spent less time socializing and in social interaction than respondents in other countries. They also spent far less time in religious activities.

American respondents in 1965 also reported unique ways of spending time. They spent more time shopping and attending church services than respondents in other countries and somewhat more time visiting and socializing. Americans also spent more time watching television and reading newspapers than respondents in other countries.

After the introduction of television, would Soviet citizens continue to spend more time (than Americans) reading books? Would they also continue to spend more time attending movies, listening to the radio and attending lectures or educational classes? Had Americans' TV viewing reached a plateau, or would they find additional programs and time to view? Would visiting and socializing continue to be as high in the United States and as low in the USSR as was suggested by findings twenty years earlier?

There was, moreover, the question of how these time-use trends are affected by demographic shifts in the population, such as increased numbers of non-married people, people without children, single parents, increasing educational levels, rising income levels or early retirement. Would today's young adults behave much as young adults did 20 years ago, or would new lifestyles develop among young adults over this period as a result of later marriages or different child-rearing patterns?

Then there were the many questions about responses to the subjective items in the questionnaire. How differently would American and Soviet citizens respond to such items, many of which were developed and formulated in an entirely different societal framework? Would the areas of time and life that satisfied Soviet citizens be similar or different from those that affected American respondents? Would the demographic and time-use factors that predict higher or lower satisfaction in one country be the same as those in the other country?

These were some of the major questions that the present study attempted to address—many of which will be analyzed in the chapters that follow. They concern topics of mutual interest in two societies that differ fundamentally in their forms of social organization, cultural values, historical orientations and behavioral assumptions. Will these forms continue to produce differing ways of spending time for their citizens? Or, are there larger, common technological and social developments that affect almost all countries in the world and that make evolving ways of spending time more similar in these two "superpowers" of the second half of the 20th century?

2

Survey Methodology

Common Study Features

As described in Chapter 1, our project basically consisted of six data collections, with three pairings across each country. The first pair of studies was conducted in 1965, the second pair in 1982–83 and the third pair in 1986. The exact study months, survey sites, sample sizes and instruments used in each of these six data collections are outlined in Table 2.1.

The central data collection instrument in each study was the time diary, as was illustrated in Table 1.1. This was an open-ended form filled in by the respondents to cover all the activities in which they had engaged on the designated diary day; that day was the day following the date of the initial contact with the respondent. Diary days were spread evenly across days of the week so they could be aggregated and generalized to a week's worth of activities. Respondents were instructed to record all their activities, starting at midnight on the designated day and running to midnight on the next day, (that is, for the full 24-hour day).

Demographic and other background information were collected in separate questionnaires. The structure of these questionnaires varied in format and size from study to study. In all three Soviet studies, respondents filled in this information themselves on self-completion forms. This was also true for the 1982–83 and 1986 American studies, but in the 1965–66 Jackson study the questions were asked and recorded by interviewers. All forms for all six studies were completed in the respondent's own home.

Basic demographic data collected in all six studies included data on the respondents' sex, age, occupation, marital status, parental status, education and residential location. Additional background questions included household amenities and appliances. Several attitude, perception and estimation questions were asked in the 1965–66 Jackson study, and a few were added in the 1965 Pskov study. A completely different set of such "subjective" questions was included in the joint American-Soviet studies in the 1980s.

These subjective questions consisted of four basic types of questions regarding various activities: frequency of participation, skill levels for

Table 2.1
Features of the Six Joint U.S.-USSR Time Use Projects

Country	Year	Months	City	Sample	Instruments
USSR	1965	(Oct.–Nov.)	Pskov	2,947	Time Diary
	1982–	(Spring)	Kerch	698	Time Diary
	1983	(Spring)	Kerch	655	Questionnaire
	1986	(Jan.–Feb.)	Pskov	2,396	Time Diary and Questionnaire
U.S.	1965	(Nov.–March)	Jackson	778	Time Diary
	1983	(Spring)	Maryland cities (3)	412	Time Diary and Questionnaire
	1986	(Feb.–May)	Jackson	844	Time Diary and Questionnaire

participation, enjoyment levels, and degree of satisfaction. These items were asked for five types of time use: work, housework, free-time activities at home, free-time activities away from home, and free time in general. (An outline that illustrates how these four types of questions relate to these general topic areas is shown in Table 2.3 later in this chapter.)

Included in this list of over 600 subjective questions were items on job involvement, job satisfaction, housework skills, division of household work among family members, satisfaction with stores and household services, frequency of social interaction, leisure activity skills and frequency, favorite television programs and music, educational and civic activities, sports skills and participation, overall planning for free-time activities, time pressures, and general goals for leisure activities. A final set of questions asked respondents about their overall life situation, their perceived standard of living and the degree of satisfaction with various aspects of their lives; these were evaluated both in current terms and in relation to how their life situation had been five years previously and was expected to be five years in the future.

In general, then, one could visualize the overall study content in terms of the various components diagrammed in the model in Figure 2.1. This model conceives of individuals as attempting to achieve satisfaction with life and its component parts through various activity pattern factors and schedules of daily activities. These, in turn, are influenced by the individual's stage in the life cycle, social status, family status, and access to

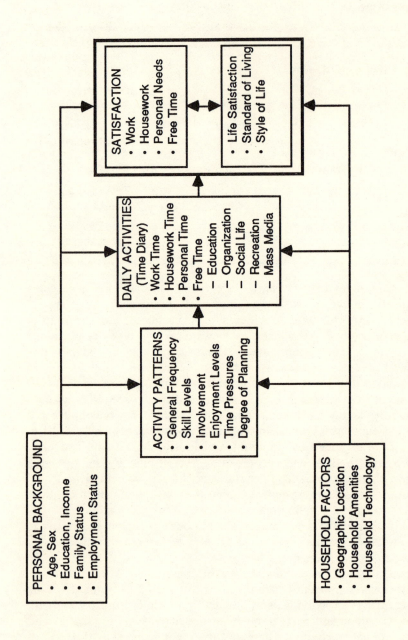

PERSONAL BACKGROUND
- Age, Sex
- Education, Income
- Family Status
- Employment Status

HOUSEHOLD FACTORS
- Geographic Location
- Household Amenities
- Household Technology

ACTIVITY PATTERNS
- General Frequency
- Skill Levels
- Involvement
- Enjoyment Levels
- Time Pressures
- Degree of Planning

DAILY ACTIVITIES
(Time Diary)
- Work Time
- Housework Time
- Personal Time
- Free Time
  - Education
  - Organization
  - Social Life
  - Recreation
  - Mass Media

SATISFACTION
- Work
- Housework
- Personal Needs
- Free Time

- Life Satisfaction
- Standard of Living
- Style of Life

Figure 2.1
A General Model Connecting the Various Study Variables

household amenities and technology. Figure 2.1 is presented as a general descriptive model that attempts some initial organization of the various survey variables, rather than a causal model that attempts to make precise predictions or explanations. As the analysis of data proceeds, this model will undergo considerable refinement and specification depending on the problems to be addressed and the specific factors that affect those individual problems.

Chapter 3 reviews the basic background and personal variables examined in the study. The basic time-use data are presented in Chapter 4. Some general bivariate analyses linking five basic demographic variables (employment status, gender, age, education and marital status) to time-use variables are also presented in Chapter 4. Chapter 5 concerns itself with the more long-term questions of how aggregate time use has changed across time.

Some initial multivariate analyses of the study's subjective variables (e.g., job and free-time satisfaction) are presented in Chapter 6. Undoubtedly many of these time-use changes can be traced to attempts on the part of individuals to increase the satisfaction they derive from their lives, or from the activities in which they engage. While it may not be possible to isolate the causal linkages between factors in long-term shifts given the present set of variables and research design, the study, nonetheless, does provide a rich set of variables and possible hypotheses for investigating these linkages and/or for examining their empirical plausibility.

Before moving on to such long-term analyses, we turn to a basic description of the time-survey sites and of the field procedures used in each site.

History and Background of Pskov

Pskov has been the center of the Pskov administrative region since 1944. As shown in Map 2.1, it is located 160 miles southwest of Leningrad at the intersection of the Velikov and Pskov rivers. The average yearly temperature in January is 19 degrees Fahrenheit and 63 degrees Fahrenheit in June.

Pskov is one of the most ancient of Russian cities, with chronicle mentions of Pskov as early as the year 903. By the 13th century, Pskov had become a feudal republic that conducted an extensive trade with the countries of Western Europe. It was united with the Russian centralized state in 1510.

As shown in Table 2.2, prior to World War II, 62,000 residents lived in Pskov. When the city was liberated from German control on 23 July 1944, the city's industrial enterprises had been totally destroyed. This included the city's power station, water system, trolley network, forty-five medical

Map 2.1
Location of Pskov

Table 2.2
Pskov Population Estimates: 1939–1986

1939	1944 (23 June)	1944 (23 Sept.)	1959	1965	1979	1986 1 Jan.
62,000	143	10,500	81,100	115,000	175,700	197,300

institutions, fifteen schools, and 200 stores; 93 percent of the city's living space also had been burned. At the moment of liberation only eighteen buildings remained undamaged in the city, and only 143 people were still registered as living in the city.[4]

After liberation, the industry of the city, its housing stock, and historical and architectural monuments were completely restored and rebuilt. Table 2.2 shows the rapid population growth of Pskov since its day of liberation. By 1965, the city had thirty-eight industrial enterprises, mainly in machinery building, construction materials, woodworking and foodstuffs.

Since the first study of time budgets of the population in 1965, Pskov has become a large industrial center in the northwest part of the Russian Republic. Almost two-thirds (65 percent) of the population is employed in industry, transport, communication or construction. Among its larger enterprises are the Pskov Electromachine Factory, the production unit, and the Pskov factory for heavy electrical welding equipment. The city has many consumer-service enterprises, offering more than thirty types of consumer services; there are four hotels, six restaurants, five cafes and nine dining halls.

Pskov has a Pedagogical Institute and a branch of the North-West Polytechnic Institute, as well as specialized secondary schools offering training in industrial, agricultural, cooperative and construction occupations; there are also cultural-educational, and professional-technical trade schools in medicine, music, etc. About 25,000 persons studied in the general and evening schools in 1985, and 1,700 students received degrees in secondary education.[5]

A total of 42,000 Pskov residents were engaged in some form of education through the schools, either at the Polytechnic, special secondary, day or evening higher educational institutions. In 1985, nearly 14,000 children attended seventy-one preschool facilities, such as nurseries, kindergartens etc.[6]

Within the city are the regional theater of drama, a 923-seat puppet theater, a planetarium, three museums, twenty-eight public libraries, three stadiums, a physical conditioning center, two swimming pools, a hippodrome, two rowing clubs, three cultural centers and one youth center. There are five movie theaters with 1,685 seats, which on the average have thirty separate film showings daily.

Intensive construction of housing units is carried on in the city. There are now about 14 square meters of usable living space per inhabitant. In 1985 alone, about 7,000 persons moved to improved living quarters and 94,300 square meters of new housing space were put into use, almost three times more than the 34,000 square meters in 1965.[7]

In terms of providing medical service to the population, Pskov has 1,100 physicians and a total of 3,000 hospital beds run by all Ministries and agencies. There are two children's hospitals with a total of 170 beds.

Pskov has increased its transport connections with other cities and regions since 1965. Twenty years ago, Aeroflot offered airline connections only with Moscow and Leningrad, along with eight local lines. By 1986, Pskov had air connection with five cities in the Russian Republic alone. Pskov is a 13-hour train ride from Moscow and a five and one-half hour ride from either Leningrad or Riga.

Along with the national newspapers, Pskov residents can read their local daily paper, *Pskovskaia Pravda*. Pskov also has its own TV station. In 1965, there were a little more than 16,000 TV sets; even with the First National Channel in operation, there were no more than twelve hours a day of programming. By 1986, however, color television broadcasts had been introduced and four channels could be received (two national, one Leningrad and one local), with a total broadcast time of more than forty-six hours a day.

Survey Procedures in Pskov

The research design involved collecting study information for the research tasks described in Chapter 1. This includes the comparison of the 1986 Pskov results with both the data from the 1965 international project and with the parallel 1986 Jackson survey.

The basic tasks of the study, then, called for three types of data, each requiring its own response form:

Form 1: Statistical data, characterizing the respondent's general living standards. (Background)

Form 2: Objective data, characterizing the resident's use of working and non-working time. (Time Diary)

Form 3: Subjective data, characterizing the respondent's opinions about the use of time. (Opinion Questionnaire)

Form 1 contained sections on general information about the respondent, information about his/her family, housing conditions, social position, and information about the diary day. The information obtained on these forms would be used first to describe the demographic composition of the sample and second to cross tabulate against information contained in the diary (Form 2) and the questionnaire (Form 3). Form 1 was either filled out by the interviewer during the first meeting with the respondent, or by the respondents themselves.

The Time Diary (Form 2) was designed to collect information characterizing people's actual behavior. In the diary, respondents recorded the times of activities they had engaged in during the course of the day, duration of these activities, simultaneously-occurring activities ("secondary" types), the location of the activities, and other people who were present. The diary was filled out for the complete days from 0:00 in the morning through 23:59 hours at night. The same format and information were recorded in the 1965 time budgets, although the form of the diary had been slightly modified to ease recording of activities.

In the diary form, respondents transcribed (in their own words) the kinds of activities they had engaged in for the (previously determined) diary day; these accounts were subsequently reviewed by the interviewer. Previous testing had shown this method gave the most exact time-use information for studies in the USSR. In order to ensure correct completion of the diary, each respondent was shown a brief instruction booklet ("Instructions to Subject about Completing the Activity Diary") which described the correct procedures for completing it, as well as an example.

Obviously, the structure of people's activity differs on different days of the week. In order to control for these large day-of-the-week differences in daily activity, an equal representation of various days of the week was designed into the sampling plan.

The third and final form, "Your Opinion About the Use of Time," included subjective questions designed to obtain general information about the respondent's way of life, including the frequency of engaging in various types of activities, preferences and enjoyment levels which may have affected the choice of one or another type of activity, favorite mass media content, skill areas, satisfactions regarding activities and so forth. These questions were grouped into the following topic sections:

- Working time (Section E)
- Housework and daily needs (Section G)
- Leisure at home (Section I1)
- Leisure and facilities for culture, leisure, sport (Section I2)
- Outdoor recreation (Section I3)
- Free time as a whole (Section I4)
- Overall evaluation of various aspects of the way of life (Section I5)

Various scales and questions were developed to examine each area in each section, as illustrated in Table 2.3.

Table 2.3
Question Numbers for Various Questionnaire Areas

Question type/Section	Housework (G)	At Home Leisure (I1)	Away-from-home Leisure (I3)	Sports and Recreation (I3)
Activity Preferences	G1	—	I14	—
Skills	G6	I3	—	I21
Frequency of participation	G3	I4	I10	I22, I23
Satisfaction	G8	I7	—	I24

In addition to this joint-study content, the Soviet Working Group investigated a number of separate technical questions. The first question concerned refining the quality of the sample and interviewing, such as the reasons why contact was not made with certain respondents, the mobility of different groups of the population, and so forth. In addition, information was obtained on any unusual conditions during the survey, the behavior of the respondent while completing the survey, and related topics. A special "Interviewer Report Form" was used for these purposes, similar to that used in previous community surveys.

The second question concerned data on the characteristics of the interviewer, both in terms of their socio-demographic background and their subjective orientations. This was used to compare with the respondent's answers to the questions on the questionnaire as well as for training purposes. In any interview situation, the possibility arises for an individual interviewer's characteristics to influence the answers the respondent gives. For this reason, as part of their training, each interviewer filled out the same questionnaire completed by the respondents. While the method of filling out the questionnaire supposes that the respondent would fill it out himself or herself, respondents were given help by the interviewer when necessary.

The Soviet part of the project also surveyed Pskov adolescents aged 12 to 17. For this part of the project, the same diary form that was used for the adults was used to record types of activity; adolescents also filled out a special questionnaire, "Youth Look at Themselves and Their Problems."

Sample Selection Procedures

The general sample frame encompassed the permanent adult population living in the city of Pskov aged 18 and older. There were to be exceptions: persons absent from Pskov for long periods of time due to work assignments, vacations and the like; on-call military personnel; hospital patients; prisoners; and temporary visitors to the city.

In 1965, the size of the survey had been established a priori by the multinational criteria. It was to include not less than 2,000 persons overall and not less than 500 persons in each city to be surveyed. The size of the sample in Pskov was set at between 2,500 and 3,000 persons, with 2,947 respondents in the final sample.

The size of the 1986 sample was also set at between 2,500 and 3,000. This was determined by the need to obtain representative data on the time use and opinions of all segments of the urban population. Earlier experience indicated that each demographic group needs to be represented by a minimum of ten to twelve people.

The basic sampling frame for the study involved voting lists. Although the lists of voters (in principle) can be a very convenient and unbiased basis for a sample of permanent residents of the city older than 18, they could not be used directly as a sampling frame, since they had not been updated for one year; thus they did not reflect the new cohort of youth who had reached 18, or the numbers who had died or had moved from Pskov. Thus, the sampling unit from these lists became the voter's address and not the voter.

The sample was implemented in three stages. In the first stage, election districts of the city served as the primary sampling unit; in the second stage, it was the family (more precisely the address of the family), and in the third stage, the immediate respondent chosen within the family.

In the *first stage* of the sample, each election district in the city was stratified into one of six historically-evolving regions of the city. These regions are significantly different in character of building and settlement, and also on a number of socio-demographic variables. The sample was stratified to ensure proportional representation of the inhabitants of each region. A systematic sample of every second election district included thirty-two of the sixty-two election districts in the final sample; in 1965 the sample included forty districts.

In the *second stage,* a list of voters (and addresses) was arranged alphabetically in each election district; the address of the family in which the survey would take place was then systematically chosen. Since the size of the election lists varied from district to district (by around 40 percent), the number of families (addresses) chosen was done in a manner to assure equal representation of each district. Thus, the sample contained a proportional number of voters from each district. The result of the second stage selection, then, was the list of addresses of families in which the survey would take place.

In the *third stage,* one respondent at each chosen address was randomly selected by the interviewer, according to the techniques described in Kish (1965). Formal techniques had to be developed, however, relating to the choice of respondents in certain unusual situations.

1. If the person chosen from the list of voters lived in a dormitory, that person was interviewed; if that person had left, the first person from the alphabetized list who lived in that room was designated as the respondent.
2. If a divorced couple still lived together because they had not yet made separate housing arrangements, they were considered a single family and the choice of respondents was made from a Kish table.
3. If the interviewer visited the family's address three times and could not locate the respondent, or if the respondent refused to participate in the survey, that family was replaced by a new one from a supplementary list.

As an indicator of the representativeness of the sample of families (the second selection stage), the proportion of the sample having particular types of housing space was calculated (private home ownership, for example). The proportion of private homes calculated from the sample was 11.3 percent. According to general administrative data, 11.2 percent of Pskov inhabitants of the city lived in such private units.

Organization of the Field Procedures

The organization of research included the following elements as part of the overall research plan:

1. Selection and training of Moscow researchers at the Institute of Sociological Research who were to supervise and conduct the research in Pskov.
2. Duplication of the research forms.
3. Identification and listing of the sample families and addresses to be used by interviewers.
4. Selection and training of Pskov interviewers to immediately collect the data.
5. Completion of field work and data collection by members of the field team.
6. Organization of the work of the interviewers.

The administrative group who directed the field work consisted of fifteen researchers from the Institute for Sociological Research. Following their training in Moscow, one part of the research administrative group arrived in Pskov on 10 January 1986 with duplicated and numbered survey instruments. The second administrative group arrived a week later. The first survey began on 16 January 1986.

The sample of families/addresses (the second stage) had been selected from voter lists several months prior to the beginning of the study. These were entered into a computer in such a way that distances from respondent to respondent for each interviewer were kept to a minimum.

Interviewer Training

The selection and training of interviewers from among the residents of the city was the most crucial element of the organization of the research. Some 360 unpaid volunteers were chosen.

Training of the interviewers was conducted in groups of 20–30 people over a two-day period. On the first day, one of the members of the administrative group explained the tasks and techniques of the research. Each interviewer was trained in matters relating to selection of respondents in the household, standardized interview procedures to be followed during the survey, initiation of contacts with the selected families, methods for selection of respondents according to the Kish table, completion of the Search Form, etc.

Familiarity with the survey instruments was achieved by means of each interviewer filling out the data form and the questionnaire during the training session. All interviewers also filled out a time diary at home by writing their activities for the diary day while at home.

The second day of training consisted of identifying and correcting mistakes in filling out the diary and explaining unclear segments in the questionnaire; procedures for the survey of children was explained, and the entire technique of the survey was reviewed again. Each interviewer received seven family addresses and the corresponding set of instruments; each was then given two weeks to complete the interviews.

Administration

The research administration was organized in four operational centers located in various parts of the city. Certain numbers of interviewers were assigned to each center in order to establish control over their field work.

After receiving their assignments for questioning seven adults (plus one adolescent), the interviewers had to undertake a selection of respondents using the procedures described above; they also had to check how well each document was filled out. For this, the interviewer had to visit the respondent several times.

The interviewer recorded the results of all visits to the families and contacts with the respondent until the successful completion of the Search

Form. If the interviewer did not succeed after three attempts to carry out the survey (due to not-at-homes, etc.), the administrative group selected the next family on the reserve list. Once the respondent agreed to the survey, the interviewer read certain questions and transcribed the responses of the respondent. If at all possible, however, the questionnaire was filled out by the respondents themselves. At the end, the interviewer explained the purpose of the time diary and reached agreement on a day the respondent would fill it out and on the date for the next meeting. Interviewers were instructed to distribute these seven adult diaries across each day of the week.

On the appointed day, the interviewers again visited the respondent. They checked the adequacy of the diary entries and, if necessary, asked that any mistakes be corrected. The interviewers then returned the completed survey forms to the administrative center. The research administrators, in turn, checked the quality of the completed forms.

As noted above, a supplemental survey of adolescents aged 12 to 17 was conducted using a special questionnaire. The adolescents were chosen from the same families in which the adults were being interviewed. In compiling the list of the members of the family, all persons aged 12 to 17 were included in a separate table. The interviewers questioned one of the first adolescents on the list whom they came to: if there were any other adolescents, the interviewer notified the research administrators, who then distributed them among those interviewers whose respondent families did not include adolescents in the proper age groups.

The questionnaire was given to the adolescent to complete in the presence of the interviewer. In connection with the techniques of selecting respondents for the sample described above, youth who lived in dormitories were not included.

Editing and Coding

Two groups of coders were trained to use the direct entry data features of the computer and to enter the data accordingly. This coding of the data was put under intensive control as described later in the details of the diary coding process.

History and Background of Jackson

Jackson is located in the state of Michigan, which is near the center of the Great Lakes region in the northern midwest area of the United States. Jackson is near the southern edge of the state near the Ohio border, and it is one of a number of small Michigan cities (e.g., Kalamazoo, Grand Rapids) lying on a major transportation corridor between Detroit (75 miles

Map 2.2
Location of Jackson

to the east) and Chicago (about 200 miles to the west), as is shown in Map 2.2.

Like the rest of the immediate area in southern Michigan, Jackson was initially settled by Americans of German and English background in the early 1800s. The first settler of the Jackson area was Horace Blackman who arrived from upstate New York (Tioga County) in July of 1829. One year later, the settlement had its first post office. The village was originally named Jacksonburgh in honor of President Andrew Jackson, but was eventually shortened to Jackson in 1833. In 1841, the Michigan Central Railroad was extended to Jackson, and the city continues to be an important railway center to this day. In July of 1854, the Republican Party was formed under some large oak trees near the present day center of town; the event was commemorated on a visit by President Howard Taft in 1910.

As shown in Table 2.4, there was a net population loss of about 5,000 people in the Jackson County area between 1980 and 1985, so that the 143,746 residents of 1985 represent virtually the same population size as in 1970. In the 1980 census, the population in the city of Jackson was 39,739, and in the Jackson urbanized area (the area covered in the present survey), the population was 81,171. The population in Jackson city in 1980 was down from a population of 45,484; this is a familiar pattern for several "Rust Belt" cities in the midwest, particularly for a city as closely tied to the automobile industry as Jackson. Changes in the county population since 1930 shown in Table 2.4 indicate that prior to the 1980s, the county's population had grown rather steadily since 1940.

Jackson lies at 1,003 feet above sea level, and the city covers about 11 square miles out of the 707 square miles in Jackson County. Jackson averages 31 inches of rainfall annually and has a temperature variation from a low of -5 to 35 degrees Fahrenheit in the winter months to highs in the low 90s in the summer. Average annual temperature is 49 degrees Fahrenheit (or 9 degrees C).

Jackson has many educational institutions. The public schools include eight schools at the elementary level, one junior high school and one senior high school. There are also twelve religious schools of varying denominations, four business and secretarial schools, six industrial technical and trade schools, and twenty preschools. There are four universities

Table 2.4
Jackson County Population Estimates: 1930–1985

1930	1940	1950	1960	1970	1980	1985
92,304	93,108	107,925	131,994	143,274	151,495	143,746

and colleges, including Jackson Community College and Spring Arbor College.

Jackson has its own planetarium, its own professional symphony orchestra, seven historical societies, three museums, thirty-seven volunteer organizations, twenty-nine parks, fifteen playlots, seventeen swimming pools or beaches, sixteen campgrounds, eighteen golf courses, eleven hotels and more than forty restaurants. There are more than one hundred places of worship, with ninety-eight Protestant churches, ten Catholic churches, a Jewish synagogue and one Eastern Orthodox church.

Although only one television station operates in Jackson, residents can receive as many as forty-three different television stations and read four locally produced newspapers. There are four local radio stations.

There is one airport offering charter service and flight training, a municipal bus system, interstate bus lines, an Amtrak railway station connecting to either Detroit or Chicago, and extensive highway facilities.

There are four central banks in Jackson and three savings and loan associations, some with branch offices; the largest bank has thirteen branch offices. There are three hospitals, one with 488 beds (and 160 staff physicians), one with 194 beds and one with seventy-five beds. There are twelve major civic organizations, including Kiwanis, Rotary and Lions Clubs.

The Jackson District Library has thirteen branches and contains more than 212,000 volumes. Jackson county contains more than 17,000 acres of park and recreation area in its twenty-nine facilities. There are tracks for harness racing and USAC and NASCAR auto racing. The illuminated Cascade Waterfalls is a main tourist attraction in the city.

Jackson's government is administered by a city manager, a mayor, and eight commissioners. Although Jackson is the county seat (see Map 2.2) and has several county administrative offices, it is mainly an industrial center. Its industrial base was one of the main reasons Jackson was chosen to be comparable to the small industrial European cities selected in the 1965 multinational time-budget project. Therefore, more of Jackson's population is employed in durable goods industries than is true for the United States as a whole.

The 1980 Jackson urbanized area was very close to 1980 Michigan state estimates in the proportion of foreign born citizens (3 percent vs. 4 percent for the state), state-born residents (75 percent vs. 76 percent), ability to speak a second language (5 percent vs. 7 percent), high school graduates (66 percent vs. 68 percent), college graduates (12 percent vs. 14 percent), children under 6 years (23 percent vs. 23 percent), under 18 living with two parents (73 percent vs. 76 percent), birth rate and median age (29.5).

Jackson was slightly lower than average in male labor force participation (63 percent vs. 75 percent for the state), but about average for women's participation (48 percent vs. 49 percent). The overall unemployment rate in 1980 was 10 percent vs. 11 percent for the state, and 14 percent of families had no workers (vs. 13 percent for the state). Median household income was $17,000 vs. $19,000 for the state, with 11 percent living in poverty (vs. 10 percent for the state).

Michigan's industrial base, and its strong ties to the automobile industry, are the main reasons why Jackson residents have experienced greater than average rates of unemployment in the 1970s and 1980s; that is also a reason for the lack of significant growth in the Jackson urban area since the 1960s.

Thus, while Jackson had seemed an ideal comparison city in the U.S. to contrast with the Soviet city of Pskov in 1965, several important differences between the two cities have arisen since 1965. Perhaps most important for the present survey was the lack of growth and generally poor economic climate in Jackson at the time of the 1986 study. Because of its lack of significant growth, it is now much smaller than the city of Pskov— as well as becoming relatively less prosperous relative to other cities in the United States.

However, neither the factor of city size nor income has been found to be an important predictor of time expenditure, which is mainly determined by sex role, education and cultural factors. However, employment status is a major factor and is, therefore, a major control variable in our analyses. Moreover, with the availability of 1985 national time-use data, it again becomes possible to verify whether or not changes found in Jackson hold in other parts of the U.S. as well.

In order to reduce project costs, the 1986 study differed in that only the urbanized area of Jackson was included. It is possible, however, to exclude the more rural part of the 1965 sample for more direct comparison purposes. It was also the case that the urban-rural differences in the 1965–66 study were not great.

Sample Selection Procedures

The project data in Jackson were collected by means of two self-completion forms filled out by the 844 respondents in the study: the time diary and the 36-page questionnaire.

Probability sampling methods were employed to initially identify respondents in both personal and telephone contact modes. However, respondents in both contact modes personally filled out both the questionnaires and the time diaries on self-completion forms. These forms were then personally reviewed and collected by interviewers on the day after the designated diary day.

Households were selected by probability sampling techniques for the two contact modes as follows.

1. *Personal contact mode (511 respondents).* The basic sampling frame was the urbanized area of Jackson as defined by the 1984 edition of the R.L. Polk City directory. That directory was updated from a 1982 city directory mainly by means of self-completion forms delivered to each housing unit in the Jackson urban area. As in most city directories, each household address in the directory is listed along with the identity and telephone number of the occupant of that address as identified by the information returned to R. L. Polk; if no information was obtained about that address, it was listed as vacant in the directory.

However, the sole piece of information used to select the sample was the designated address as listed on chosen lines from the directory. Lines were chosen based on a sampling frame that first implicitly stratified all entries in the directory and then systematically selected blocks or combinations of those lines at random. Thus, the first step in the sample selection was a count of the nearly 40,000 lines on the 338 pages in the directory.

Given the desired sample size of approximately 500 households (with one respondent per household), an initial sample of lines was drawn to yield the desired number of households. This was accomplished by a systematic, clustered sample as follows. A cluster size of fifteen lines was designated, and after a randomly designated line was identified, all listed addresses in the next fourteen lines were included in the sample. On average, it was found that fifteen lines yielded the appropriate number of actual addresses of *housing* units (not businesses or other buildings). Only the first line of the address was included in the sample, so that each address had the same chance of being included in the sample, and so that listings spanning two or three lines were not overrepresented.

In order to cover housing units not listed in the directory, interviewers did check in the field to ensure that there were no missing addresses that should have been listed in the directory. That included addresses between the last listed addresses in the selected cluster and the next listed address in the directory, by using the "half-open interval" technique.

Therefore, to obtain the desired number of households, a large selection of clustered blocks was made to yield the desired number of addresses on the directory lines by the interval; this yielded the random interval to select every nth line. The first line was identified by a random number chosen between 1 and n, which was k. That meant that line k was the first line drawn into the sample, and the next 14 lines fell into the sample as well. All addresses in these lines were then included in the sample, if that address's first listing line was in the interval k and k + 14.

The next cluster of lines selected into the sample were those starting with line k plus the interval n. That meant that addresses on the next 14 lines (n + k + 14) fell into the sample.

With the final selection, therefore, the expected number of lines to yield the desired number of household addresses had been identified. These were the addresses, then, at which the interviewers made an initial contact to identify a randomly chosen respondent to be included into the sample.

The respondent was then chosen at random by the household selection methods described in Kish (1965). Effectively, all respondents over age 18 were listed by sex and by age (oldest males first, etc. through the youngest female), and one adult was chosen at random from this listing. If that respondent was not at home, the interviewer made an appointment to return to that sample respondent to describe the diary and questionnaire forms and how they were to be completed by that sample respondent. A sample diary form was left to illustrate further how the diary was to be completed. Interviewers reviewed the material with each respondent before they left to ensure the respondent understood how to complete the form. Interviewers then returned two days later to ensure that the forms had been filled out correctly and to fill in any gaps. They also gave respondents the payment form for the incentive they were promised as a reward for participation.

2. *Telephone mode (333 respondents).* In this sample, the random-digit-dial method of selecting households was employed. The initial sample frame consisted of the first five digits of telephone exchanges selected randomly from addresses in the Polk City directory. Two numbers were then added to identify a list of randomly-designated complete numbers. That number was called and a determination was attempted by the telephone interviewer as to whether that household address was inside the Jackson city limits or was otherwise part of the Jackson urbanized area as defined in the city directory.

If that household appeared to be one that would be listed in the Jackson urban area, the interviewer asked to speak to a randomly-designated household member. The member chosen (male or female, old or young) depended on a random predesignation for that household. Once that household member was identified at random, s/he was asked to complete a time diary for the prior day; if the respondent was not at home, the interviewer called back later at a prescheduled time to complete the diary for the prior day.

The time diary was collected by first asking respondents what they had been doing at 12 o'clock (midnight) on the prior day, then what activity they had done after this activity, then the next activity, and so forth, until the respondent had accounted for the full 24 hours of the day. At that point the interviewer told the respondent about the need to collect another day's time account and to complete the household questionnaire. The respondent's address was identified in order to mail the diary and questionnaire to that address.

If the telephone respondent agreed to participate, questionnaire and instruction sheets were sent to that respondent. That address was checked against the Polk City directory listings to be sure it was actually in the urbanized Jackson area. Respondents were contacted six days later to ensure that the forms had arrived and to review instructions for completion of both. They were also told about the interviewer who would be arriving two days later to pick up the completed forms.

As an incentive to participate in both contact modes, respondents were offered $10 for their cooperation in completing the forms. This did serve to increase initial levels of respondent cooperation and interest in the study. However, as many respondents found that the forms took them several hours to complete, their initial enthusiasm waned, sometimes resulting in large blocks of missing time periods in the diaries and large segments of the questions not being completed. While interviewers were able to fill in much of this missing information on their second (final) visit, many respondents were unwilling to cooperate in providing complete information. Their partial responses were included in the final data collection to increase sample coverage.

Interviewer Training

For the Jackson study, a total of eleven interviewers were used for the on-site portion of the study. The supervisor of the interviewing team had personally distributed and collected all of the interviews in the pilot-test phase of the Jackson survey procedures in November and December of 1985, by collecting diary and questionnaire data from twenty-five respondents in that pilot test.

He then personally observed the data collection organization and procedures in Pskov and held several days of discussion with his interviewing supervisor counterpart for the Soviet data collection. By being present during the actual data collection in Pskov, he was able to ensure that the data collection procedures used in Jackson would be as comparable as possible.

At the same time, there were to be clear differences in the procedures used in the two countries, mainly because of the restricted funding available for the U.S. data collection. Thus the Jackson data collection:

1. Involved far fewer interviewers and took longer field time to complete (although 80 percent of the survey interviews were completed within two months).

2. Involved far less contact time with each respondent. Basically, once the selected respondent in the household was identified, the interviewer showed him/her the two forms and briefly described how each form was to be filled out; a sample diary form was left behind to illustrate to the respondent the level of detail required. This contact time ranged from 5 to 15 minutes, depending on how well the respondent appeared to understand the interview forms.
3. Left more discretion for respondents in interpreting questions on their own; this also meant that there would be more missing data.
4. Had much less "official" status and implied reasons for respondent cooperation.

Thus, Jackson interviewers had minimal time to establish rapport with respondents and to explain difficult or unusual questions to them.

All interviewers underwent a four-hour training session in which they were trained in sampling and respondent selection methods. The supervisor often accompanied the interviewers in the field to ensure further data standardization. Interviewers themselves filled out the diary and questionnaire forms to become thoroughly acquainted with the task expected of their respondents. All completed forms were reviewed not only by the interviewer on his/her return visit, but by the supervisor to ensure they were filled out completely and correctly.

Diary Data Collection

As can be seen from the sample diary page in Chapter 1, the time diary form remained basically the same as that used in the 1965 and 1983 studies. In order to illustrate to respondents the types of activities and level of detail we were expecting of them in completing their diaries, an example of a completed diary form was given to them or enclosed in each packet mailed to them. That example form was filled out in considerable detail, with several hand-written comments by the fictitious "diary keeper" to help the interpretation of unusual diary entries (e.g., going home during work; caring for children while playing sports). In general, this was intended to ensure that respondents would include enough detail in their diaries; that measure seems to have been successful in that the 1986 diaries contained about the same average number of primary activities (about twenty-five) as was the case in the 1965–66 "tomorrow" diaries.

Coding

Once received and checked, these diaries were then entered into a PDP1144 computer in College Park, Maryland, by a trained coding staff using the direct data entry features of the University of California at Berkeley Computer Assisted Telephone Interviewing (CATI) system. Activities were coded into one of 271 activity codes, which had been expanded from the 174 categories developed at the University of Michigan for the 1975 data. This in turn represented an expansion of the ninety-six basic code categories that Szalai et al. (1972) had developed for the 1965 Multinational Time-Use Project and which formed the basis of the Soviet activity coding as well. That basic two digit coding scheme is shown in Figure 2.2

This 96-category scheme had been developed on the basis of classifications of activity developed by researchers in the Soviet Union. The scheme first subdivides activities into *paid work* codes (codes 00–09), *family care* (codes 10–39) and *personal-care* activities (codes 40–49). Freetime activities are also subdivided into five general categories. More finegrained distinctions within these ten categories are reflected in the second digit of this code, and, as noted above, the code for this project has been expanded to the 271 categories to reflect further distinctions within activities.

All coders were extensively trained on this code category system and followed the same set of coding conventions that had been used in the 1966 study, and which had been elaborated by the Survey Research Center at the University of Michigan for its 1975 time-use diary project. That scheme was further expanded after several days of joint coding discussions between the American and Soviet researchers in preparation for the present project, so that many of the 200 + coding distinctions used by the Soviet side would be maintained in the U.S. detailed code. In order to check on the correspondence of these coding procedures, we plan to have coders at the University of Maryland and coders at the Institute for Sociological Research recode a subset of fifty diaries from the two studies independently.

As in Pskov, each activity in the Jackson diary was coded descriptively as a separate record using a three-digit code. In coding the Jackson data, however, the time the activity began and ended was also coded in four-digit international time (e.g., 8 AM = 0800; 8 PM = 2000), as well as the location of the activity digit), the social partners who were present (two digits) and any secondary activities (three digits). When this 17-digit data entry for all activities in the diary had been entered and computed, the totals were computer checked to ensure that each day's diary entries added to exactly 1,440 minutes (24.0 hours). These "variable-field" data (i.e. varying depending on the number of activities reported) were then processed by a special computer program to provide "fixed-field" compilations of diary time spent on ninety-six activities for each activity, i.e. total daily minutes spent working, cooking, watching TV, etc., for that

Working and related time (00–09)		Adult education and training (50–59)	
00	Regular work	50	Attend school
01	Work at home	51	Other classes
02	Overtime	52	Special lecture
03	Travel for job	53	Political courses
04	Waiting, delays	54	Homework
05	Second job	55	Read to learn
06	Meals at work	56	Other study
07	At work, other	57	Blank
08	Work breaks	58	Blank
09	Travel to job	59	Travel, study
Domestic work (10–19)		Organizational activities (60–69)	
10	Prepare food	60	Union, politics
11	Meal cleanup	61	Work as officer
12	Clean house	62	Other participation
13	Outdoor chores	63	Civic activities
14	Laundry, ironing	64	Religious organization
15	Clothes upkeep	65	Religious practice
16	Other upkeep	66	Factory council
17	Gardening, animal care	67	Misc. organization
18	Heat, water	68	Other organization
19	Other duties	69	Travel, organization
Care to children (20–29)		Spectacles, entertainment, social life (70–79)	
20	Baby care	70	Sports event
21	Child care	71	Mass culture
22	Help on homework	72	Movies
23	Talk to children	73	Theatre
24	Outdoor playing	74	Museums
25	Child health	75	Visiting with friends
26	Other, babysit	76	Party, meals
27	Other, child, relative	77	Cafe, pubs
28	Blank	78	Other social
29	Travel with child	79	Travel, organization
Purchasing of Goods (30–39)		Recreation (80–89)	
30	Marketing	80	Active sports
31	Shopping	81	Fishing, hiking
32	Personal care	82	Taking a walk
33	Medical care	83	Hobbies
34	Administrative service	84	Ladies hobbies
35	Repair service	85	Art work
36	Waiting in line	86	Making music
37	Other service	87	Parlor games
38	Blank	88	Other pastime
39	Travel, service	89	Travel, pastime
Private needs: meals, sleep (40–49)		Communication (90–99)	
40	Personal hygiene	90	Radio
41	Personal medical	91	TV
42	Care to adults	92	Play records
43	Meals, snacks	93	Read book
44	Restaurant meals	94	Read magazine
45	Night sleep	95	Read paper
46	Daytime sleep	96	Conversation
47	Resting	97	Leters, private
48	Private, other	98	Relax, think
49	Travel, personal	99	Travel, leisure

Figure 2.2
Complete Two-digit Activity Code

respondent for that day. It is the averages of these fixed-field totals that are presented in the analytic tables in the following chapters.

The time-use data in the tables that follow are also weighted by day of the week and by the demographic factors of sex and age to ensure that all days of the week are equally represented in these tables and that the overall sample figures correspond to 1980 U.S. Census Bureau figures on these factors for the U.S. data.

Thus the field and data processing procedures in the two sites were made as exactly comparable as was possible. Not only were respondents asked essentially the same questions in the same format, but identical coding and analysis procedures were used as well. The results of these comparisons are described in the chapters that follow.

3

Demographic and Personal Characteristics

This chapter presents data on the basic background of our survey respondents. It briefly reviews some of these overall characteristics, first for Pskov and then for Jackson.

It will be remembered that the data are presented only for respondents aged 18 to 65, and exclude all survey respondents aged 66 and older and those aged 12–17 in Pskov. The data are weighted to reflect population characteristics by age and sex so they can be compared to data from the 1965 studies in Chapter 6.

Background Factors in Pskov

Personal Factors

A total of 2,181 Pskov residents aged 18–65 were interviewed in 1986, compared to 2,947 persons aged 18–65 in 1965; the figures in this chapter thus exclude the 215 persons aged 65 and older who were also interviewed as part of the 1986 study. As the figures in Table 2.2 showed, Pskov has grown from a city of 115,000 residents to a city of 197,300 residents; at the same time the city has considerably extended its boundaries.

As can be seen in Table 3.1, some 56 percent of Pskov respondents were female and 44 percent male. In terms of age distribution, 17 percent were aged 18–24, 16 percent aged 25–29, 25 percent aged 30–39, 18 percent aged 40–49, 16 percent aged 50–59 and 7 percent aged 60–65.

Only 7 percent of Pskov residents had completed less than seven grades of formal education; 16 percent had completed 7 to 9 grades, 30 percent had completed secondary education, 27 percent some level of technical education, 4 percent some years of college education and 16 percent had completed a college education or post-graduate education.

About seven in ten (72 percent) of Pskov respondents were married, 15 percent were single or never married, 5 percent were widowed and about 9 percent divorced or separated. Some 8 percent of Pskov respondents lived alone, 18 percent only with a wife or husband, 42 percent with a spouse and children, 5 percent with a spouse and other relations, 8 percent with

Table 3.1
Personal Background Information on Pskov Respondents
(Entries may not add to 100% due to rounding)

Indicators	18–65 years old			Employed		
	Total	Male	Female	Total	Male	Female
Sample:						
non-weighted	2181	875	1306	1853	797	1056
weighted	3326	1448	1877	2823	1313	1510
	100%	44%	56%	100%	47%	54%
Age:						
18–24	17	14	21	14	11	17
25–29	16	17	15	17	18	16
30–39	25	27	24	28	30	27
40–49	18	19	18	21	20	21
50–54	8	10	7	9	10	8
55–59	8	8	9	7	8	7
60–65	7	6	7	4	4	4
Education:						
4–6 Grades	7	7	7	6	7	5
7–9 Grades	16	18	14	16	18	14
10–11 Grades	30	36	26	32	37	28
Technical School	27	20	32	27	20	33
Some College	4	4	4	2	3	2
College Graduate	16	15	16	17	15	18
Marital Status:						
Married	72	82	66	73	84	65
Divorced	8	5	10	8	5	11
Separated, but not						
divorced	1	*	2	1	*	2
Widowed	5	1	8	5	1	8
Single mother	1	0	1	1	0	1
Never married	14	12	12	12	10	14
With whom do you live and keep house?						
I live alone	8	6	9	8	6	10
With wife (husband)						
and no children	18	20	16	18	19	15
With wife (husband)						
and children	42	49	36	45	52	38
With wife (husband),						
parents, or other						
relatives	5	5	5	5	5	5

Table 3.1—continued

Indicators	18–65 years old			Employed		
	Total	Male	Female	Total	Male	Female
With wife (husband), children, parents, and other relatives	8	7	8	7	7	7
With parents and other relatives	12	11	13	10	9	11
With a child (no wife or husband)	5	1	8	5	1	9
With a child (or children) and parents (one of them)	2	*	1	2	*	4
Other	1	2	1	1	1	2
Position in family:						
Head of family	51	68	38	55	69	42
Spouse of the head of family	27	12	39	26	12	39
Son/daughter of head of family (or his or her spouse)	14	13	14	11	11	12
Parent of head of family	2	1	3	2	1	3
Relative	1	1	2	1	1	2
Houseworker (live-in)	*	*	*	*	*	*
Other	4	5	3	4	5	3
Persons in houshold:						
One	8	6	9	8	6	10
Two	21	19	23	20	17	22
Three	33	34	31	34	36	32
Four	26	29	24	27	29	25
Five	8	7	9	7	7	7
Six or more	5	5	4	5	5	4
Number of people who work in your household?						
One	22	17	26	20	15	23
Two	56	60	51	59	62	55
Three	14	15	14	15	16	15
Four	6	5	6	6	5	6
Five	1	1	1	1	1	1
Six or more	0	2	3	*	*	0

Table 3.1—continued

Indicators	18–65 years old			Employed		
	Total	Male	Female	Total	Male	Female
Type of Living Quarters:						
Apartment building	84	—	—	83	—	—
Townhouse for						
1–2 families	4	—	—	5	—	—
Single detached						
house	5	—	—	5	—	—
Dormitory, other	7	—	—	8	—	—
Home is located:						
In the city limits	42	—	—	4	—	—
In the industrial						
suburbs	28	—	—	29	—	—
In the non-industrial						
suburb	28	—	—	29	—	—
Other	1	—	—	1	—	—
How far is home from the center of town?						
Less than 1 kilometer	32	—	—	32	—	—
1–2 kilometers	29	—	—	29	—	—
2–5 kilometers	32	—	—	33	—	—
5–10 kilometers	5	—	—	5	—	—
10–20 kilometers	2	—	—	2	—	—
20 or more kilometers	—	—	—	—	—	—
Facilities in house/apartment:						
Running water	90	—	—	90	—	—
Gas	93	—	—	93	—	—
Sewage disposal	88	—	—	89	—	—
Central heating	86	—	—	86		
Electricity	99	—	—	99	—	—
Bath (shower)	82	—	—	82	—	—

*Less than 0.5%

an extended family (spouse, children and other relatives), 12 percent with parents and other relations, 5 percent with a child only, 2 percent with a child and parents and 1 percent with other household configurations. More than half (51 percent) of the respondents described themselves as the head of the household, 27 percent as the spouse of the head, 14 percent as a child of the head, 2 percent as the parent of the head, 1 percent as a relative and 4 percent in other categories.

In terms of total household size, 8 percent lived alone, 21 percent with one other person, 33 percent with three other people, 26 percent with four other people and 13 percent with five or more other people. More than four in ten (43 percent) respondents said they had no children in the household under age 18, 35 percent had one child, 20 percent two children, 2 percent three children and 1 percent four or more children. Less than 2 percent of respondents reported no workers in the household, with 22 percent reporting one worker, 55 percent two workers, 14 percent three workers, 6 percent four workers, and 1 percent five workers.

Some 84 percent of Pskov respondents lived in an apartment building, 4 percent in a townhouse of one or two units, 5 percent in a single detached house and 7 percent in some other type of housing unit. About 42 percent of the units were in the central part of the city of Pskov, 28 percent in the industrial areas within the city boundaries and 28 percent in the non-industrial parts of the city. Almost a third (32 percent) of Pskov respondents lived within a kilometer (0.6 mile) of the center of the city, 29 percent within 1 to 2 kilometers, 32 percent within 2 to 5 kilometers, 5 percent within 5 and 10 kilometers and 2 percent between 10 and 20 kilometers away from the city's center.

In terms of basic household amenities, 90 percent of Pskov respondents had running water in the household, 93 percent gas, 88 percent sewage disposal, 86 percent central heating, 99 percent electricity and 82 percent a bath or shower. In addition, 40 percent had some plot of land for producing food or raising animals, with 8 percent having such land at or near the house, 3 percent at a private lot away from the house, 15 percent in a gardening association or cooperative, 11 percent at a summer cottage, and 3 percent in some other arrangement.

In terms of household appliances, 95 percent of Pskov residents had a gas stove, 3 percent an electric range and 1 percent a microwave oven. In addition, 95 percent had a refrigerator, 2 percent a food processor, 6 percent a dishwasher, 14 percent an electric juice squeezer, 13 percent an electric or other electric juice cooker, 34 percent a coffee grinder or coffee maker and 77 percent some type of equipment for canning or preserving foods.

Four in five (80 percent) Pskov respondents had a washing machine, 73 percent a vacuum cleaner, 2 percent a floor polisher, 67 percent a sewing machine and 5 percent a knitting machine. A quarter (25 percent) of respondents had a gas or electric water heater, and 23 percent had a telephone.

In terms of material goods related to culture and leisure activities, 41 percent of Pskov residents had a personal library with more than 100 books. Some 98 percent of households had TV sets (73 percent had a black-and-white television set, 42 percent a color TV), and 1 percent a video recorder; 76 percent had a non-component radio, 57 percent a record player, 16 percent a component stereo system and 54 percent an (audio) tape recorder. In terms of musical instruments, 8 percent had a piano, 12 percent an accordion, 20 percent a guitar and 4 percent some other musical instrument.

Almost six in ten (57 percent) Pskov respondents had some form of sports equipment, 48 percent a work bench or collection of tools, 43 percent a still or movie camera, 71 percent a chess or checker set, 56 percent other table games and 18 percent a pocket calculator.

Employment Factors

Various aspects of the employment and occupational background of respondents are also shown in Table 3.2. Basic employment factors are shown in the first part of Table 3.2 for the entire sample aged 18 to 65, with the remaining parts of Table 3.2 referring to only those respondents identified as employed for pay, as indicated in the first line of Table 3.2. That includes about 85 percent of Pskov respondents (n = 2181).

In addition to the higher proportion of men (91 percent) who are employed than women (80 percent), there are slightly higher proportions of men than women who are disabled and who are between jobs. Higher proportions of women than men are retired (8 percent vs. 3 percent) and are temporarily off work because of maternity leave etc. (5 percent); only 1 percent of Pskov women between the ages of 18–65 list their occupation as housewife.

Some 40 percent of workers in Pskov are in manufacturing industries, 12 percent in construction, 6 percent in non-public transportation/communication and 6 percent in trade. A large proportion of Pskov's male workforce is involved in manufacturing, construction and transportation. A large proportion of the female workforce is in trade and retail, food and consumer industries, health, and education.

More than half of the workforce in Pskov can be found in "blue-collar" jobs, with 19 percent in low skilled jobs and 20 percent in semi-skilled jobs. More than 20 percent of the workforce is also in technical/engineering jobs and in white-collar/clerical jobs—most of these requiring at least some college education. Men are more likely to be employed in semi-skilled and skilled blue collar jobs, while women are far more likely than men to be employed in cleaning and white-collar/clerical jobs. Women are also somewhat more likely than men to be employed in technical jobs.

More than 80 percent of Pskov male and female workers work a five-day workweek, and less than 10 percent work six days a week. More than 80 percent work a single day shift. More than a quarter of Pskov respondents live within one kilometer of their workplace and 45 percent within two kilometers (1.2 miles); only 15 percent live more than 6 kilometers (4

Table 3.2
Employment Background of Pskov Respondents
(Totals may exceed 100% due to rounding.)

(n=)	Pskov (2181)	Male (875)	Female (1306)
Employment Status			
Employed for pay	85	91	80
Retired	6	3	8
Disabled	1	2	1
Housewife	1	0	1
Maternity	3	0	5
Other	4	4	4
	100%	100%	100%
EMPLOYED PERSONS:			
Branch of Economy			
(n=)	(1853)	(797)	(1056)
Manufacturing	40	43	38
Agriculture	3	4	3
Construction	12	16	8
Public transport	4	5	2
Other transport	6	9	4
Housing, utilities	5	5	4
Financial	1	*	1
Trade, retail	6	3	8
Food	3	1	5
Consumer	3	1	4
Health	5	2	8
Science	1	1	2
Culture, art	2	1	2
Education	4	1	6
Civic, gov't.	4	3	4
Other	2	4	*
	100%	100%	100%
Level			
Low skill	19	18	18
Semi-skilled	20	32	9
Skilled	7	14	1
Apprentice	6	6	7
Cleaning	5	1	5
Technical-college	19	16	21
no college	2	1	2
Farm			6
Other	2	2	1

Table 3.2—continued

(n=)	Pskov (2181)	Male (875)	Female (1306)
White collar			
college	17	7	25
no college	4	2	6
	100%	100%	100%
Workweek			
Six days	9	7	10
Five days	83	84	82
Four days	1	1	1
Other, varied	8	8	7
	100%	100%	100%

* Less than 0.5%

miles) away from their workplace. Thus, it is possible for almost half (48 percent) of Pskov workers to walk to work, while another 42 percent use public transportation and another 10 percent use some form of company transport.

Except for the slightly higher proportion of Pskov employed men who use company transportation, there are no notable differences between Pskov men and women regarding any of these occupational factors.

Background Factors in Jackson

Personal Factors

The basic background data on the respondents in the Jackson survey are shown in Table 3.3. This information has been weighted to reflect the age and sex 1980 Census Bureau distributions of these two characteristics. Data for the 127 respondents over the age of 65 have been excluded.

It can be seen that there is a slightly higher proportion of women (54 percent) than men (46 percent) in Jackson. The weighted age distribution was 22 percent for age 18–24, 14 percent for age 25–29, 19 percent for age 30–39, 17 percent for age 40–49, 16 percent for age 50–59 and 12 percent age 60–65.

Some 91 percent of the sample was white, 7 percent black, 4 percent Hispanic, while the remaining 2 percent was of Oriental or other background. Only 16 percent of the sample had not completed high school (that is, they had 0 to 11 years of formal education), 35 percent were high school

Table 3.3
Personal Background Information on Jackson Respondents
(Entries may not add to 100% due to rounding)

P1. Sex
46   1. Male
<u>54</u>   2. Female
100

P2. Age
22   18–24
14   25–29
19   30–39
17   40–49
16   50–59
<u>12</u>   60–65
100

P3. Race
91   1. White
7   2. Black
1   3. Oriental
8   4. Hispanic
<u>1</u>   5. Other (specify)
100

P4. Education
*   1. None
2   2. Grade School (1–8 years)
13   3. Some High School (9–11 years)
35   4. High School Graduate (12 years)
35   5. Some College Graduate (13–15 years)
9   6. College Graduate (16 years)
<u>6</u>   7. Post-Graduate Education (17+ years)
100

P5. Marital Status
58   1. Married
12   2. Divorced
3   3. Separated, but not divorced
4   4. Widowed
3   5. Single mother
20   6. Never married
<u>*</u>   7. Other (write in)
100

P6. With whom do you live and keep house?
17   1. I live alone
19   2. With wife (husband) and no children
35   3. With wife (husband) and children
*   4. With wife (husband), parents, or other relatives
*   5. With wife (husband), children, parents and other relatives
6   6. With parents and other relatives
8   7. With a child (no wife or husband)
2   8. With a child (or children) and parents (one of them)
<u>11</u>   9. Other
100

P7. Position in Family
55   1. Head of family
29   2. Spouse of the head of family
8   3. Son/daughter of head of family (or his or her spouse)
1   4. Parent of head of family
1   5. Relative
0   6. Houseworker (live-in)
<u>7</u>   7. Other
100

P8. Persons in Household
16   1. One
31   2. Two
21   3. Three
20   4. Four
8   5. Five
<u>4</u>   6. Six or more
100

Table 3.3—continued

	P9. Children under 18: How many?
48	None
13	One
21	Two
7	Three
11	Four or more
100	

	P10. Number of people who work in your household
16	None
38	One
36	Two
7	Three
2	Four
1	Five
*	Six or more
100	

	P11. Type of Living Quarters
22	1. Apartment building
5	2. Townhouse for 1–2 families
65	3. Single detached house
0	4. Dormitory
7	5. Other
100	

	P12. Home is located?
47	1. In the city limits
8	2. In the industrial suburbs
38	3. In the non-industrial suburbs
7	4. Other
100	

	P16. Home from the center of town?
15	1. Less than 1/2 mile
20	2. 1/2–1 mile
30	3. 1–3 miles
25	4. 3–6 miles
9	5. 6–12 miles
1	6. 12+ miles
100	

	P17. Facilities in your house/apartment?
98	1. Running water
89	2. Gas
82	3. Sewage disposal
82	4. Central heating
98	5. Electricity
98	6. Bath (shower)

	P18. Plot of land to grow vegetables, fruits; keep domestic animals?
52	1. No plot of land
41	2. Have—near house
4	3. Have—private, away from house
1	4. I am in a gardening co-op, etc.
2	5. Have a summer cottage with a plot of land
6	6. Other

	P19. Family has any of the following facilities?
79	1. Basement/cellar
23	2. Barn (shed)
64	3. Garage

	P20. Have the following equipment or facilities for your use?
73	1. Self-service laundry for drying and ironing laundry
52	2. Facilities for handiwork: carpentry, locksmith, other
52	3. Room for holding parties, banquets and other holidays
37	4. Children's playroom banquets and other holidays

Table 3.3—continued

	P21a. Household Appliances		P21c. Culture and Leisure
61	1. Gas stove	38	24. Personal library (with more than 100 books)
57	2. Full-size electric range		
38	3. Microwave oven	52	25. Black and white TV
99	4. Refrigerator	89	26. Color TV
32	5. Food processor	44	27. Radio (without sep- arate speakers or other components)
39	6. Dishwasher		
9	7. Electric juice squeezer		
3	8. Juice cooker (hot drink machine)	57	28. Video cassette recorder (VCR)
57	9. Coffee grinder, Coffee- maker	77	29. Tape recorder
		83	30. Record player
40	10. Equipment for canning, preserving	65	31. Stereo tuner
		66	32. Stereo amplifer and speakers
75	11. Washing machine		
92	12. Vacuum cleaner	21	33. Piano
20	13. Floor-polisher	5	34. Accordian
62	14. Sewing machine	20	35. Guitar
5	15. Knitting machine	31	36. Other musical instruments
97	16. Gas or electric water- heater		
		62	37. Sports equipment (for hunting and fishing)
96	17. Telephone		
72	18. Clothes dryer	67	38. Work-bench, collection of tools
	P21b. Means of Transportation		
		75	39. Camera or movie camera
64	19. Bicycle (adult)		
22	20. Motorcycle, motor bike, moped	61	40. Chess, checkers set
		66	41. Table games (dominoes, bingo, etc.)
94	21. Car How many?___		
21	22. Rowboat, kayak, etc.		
24	23. Motorboat	83	42. Pocket calculator (electronic)
		75	43. Washing machine
		83	42. Pocket calculator (electronic)

*Less than 0.5%.

graduates, 35 percent had some college education and 15 percent had graduated from college, while 6 percent had some post-graduate education, as well.

Almost three out of five (58 percent) respondents were married, 12 percent were divorced and 20 percent had never married. Thus, 17 percent of respondents lived alone, 19 percent lived with a spouse but without children, 10 percent with a child and no spouse and 35 percent with a spouse and children; some 11 percent described other household arrangements, mainly non-married and unrelated people sharing apartments and houses. Some 55 percent of respondents described themselves as the head of the family unit, 29 percent as the spouse of the family head and 8 percent as the child of the family head; the remaining 9 percent were again mainly unrelated roommates.

About 16 percent of respondents reported that they were the only person living in the housing unit, 31 percent said there were two persons living in the housing unit, 21 percent three, 20 percent four and the remaining 12 percent five or more. Almost half (48 percent) reported no children in the household, 13 percent one child, 21 percent two children and 18 percent three or more children; almost a quarter (23 percent) reported a child under the age of six, and 7 percent two or more children under the age of six.

Some 16 percent of respondents reported no one with paid employment in the household; 38 percent reported one worker, 36 percent two workers and 10 percent three or more workers. The median monthly income for the family was $1,600, which is about $19,000 per year; this figure included pensions, child support and other income sources besides work salary. Almost half (46 percent) rated this income as "not enough," and only 5 percent said it was more than enough. (These data are not shown in Table 3.3.)

About two-thirds (65 percent) of respondents reported living in a single-family house, 22 percent in an apartment building, 5 percent in a townhouse and 7 percent in a mobile home or some other type of housing unit. Almost half (47 percent) were located within the city limits of Jackson, the remaining 53 percent in the suburbs. Some 15 percent reported living within half a mile (just under one kilometer) from the center of the city, 20 percent between half a mile and one mile, 30 percent one to three miles, 25 percent three to six miles and 10 percent more than six miles from the city center of Jackson.

Turning to the facilities and technology available to these respondents, some 98 percent had running water, 89 percent piped-in natural gas, 82 percent sewage disposal (this figure is probably low because some respondents may have interpreted this as a garbage disposal unit), 82 percent central heating, 98 percent electricity and 98 percent a bath or shower unit.

More than half of the sample reported that they had no land area that they used to grow food or keep pets or animals; 41 percent said they had such land on or very near their property, while 6 percent or more had such land for gardening some distance away from their household property (multiple ownership was possible). Some (79 percent) reported they had a basement or cellar, 23 percent a barn or shed and 64 percent a garage. Almost three-quarters of respondents (73 percent) reported having self-service laundry facilities, 52 percent facilities for do-it-yourself activities, 52 percent facilities for entertaining and parties and 37 percent a room in which children could play.

Concerning the information that was obtained from respondents on more than forty separate types of home appliances and leisure technology, almost all respondents had an oven and 99 percent had a refrigerator. Some 38 percent had a microwave oven.

Almost four in ten (39 percent) respondents reported having a dishwasher. Almost a third (32 percent) said they had a food processor, 9 percent an electric juice machine and 3 percent a juice cooker. More than half (57 percent) reported having some type of coffee machine, and 40 percent had equipment for canning and preserving fruit and vegetable products.

Turning to other labor-saving devices, 75 percent said they had a washing machine on the premises and 72 percent an electric clothes dryer. More than nine in ten (92 percent) had a vacuum cleaner, 62 percent a sewing machine, 20 percent a floor polisher and 5 percent a knitting machine.

Almost all respondents had access to a telephone (96 percent) as well as to a gas or electric water heater (97 percent). Almost all respondents (94 percent) had access to an automobile. More than one respondent in five had either a self-propelled boat (21 percent) or motorboat (24 percent).

Almost four out of ten respondents (38 percent) reported having a personal library with more than 100 books. Almost all respondents reported having a television set, with 89 percent having a color set. More than half (57 percent) also said they had a video cassette recorder. Almost all respondents also had a radio, although only 44 percent said that radio was a stand-alone unit with enclosed speakers. Far more (66 percent) had component stereo equipment with a radio tuner. Some 83 percent had record players and 77 percent an audio tape recorder.

Ownership or access to musical equipment was far less common. About one in five respondents (21 percent) had a piano and 5 percent an accordion. More than a third (31 percent) said they had other musical instruments, which could include harmonicas, electronic keyboard units and percussion instruments.

Almost two-thirds of respondents (62 percent) said they had some type of outdoor sports equipment for skiing, camping, hunting or fishing. More than two-thirds (67 percent) said they had a work bench or a collection of tools.

Three-quarters (75 percent) of respondents had a camera or movie camera and 83 percent a pocket calculator. Close to two-thirds of respondents (66 percent) said they had table games or game sets, with 61 percent having sets for playing checkers or chess.

Employment Factors

As shown in Table 3.4, higher proportions of Jackson men (85 percent) than Jackson women (58 percent) work. Some 23 percent of Jackson women are housewives and 3 percent are on maternity or other work leave; otherwise male-female differences in retired, disabled etc. status are very close.

The largest employers of Jackson workers are manufacturing concerns, which employ just over a quarter of the Jackson workforce, with 9 percent in retail and trade, 8 percent in health, and 8 percent in education. Some 17 percent of Jackson respondents could not place themselves in any of these sectors of the economy. More men are employed in manufacturing, transportation and construction industries and more women in health, consumer and education occupations.

More than half of Jackson's employed people work in technical and white-collar jobs. Most (69 percent) of Jackson's men and women work a five-day week; however, 14 percent (21 percent among men) work a six-day week, 5 percent (9 percent among women) a four-day week and 12 percent a variable workweek. About two-thirds of workers (71 percent of men vs. 62 percent women) work a single day shift, 5 percent two shifts, 3 percent three shifts and 26 percent variable or "other" shifts. Less than 15 percent of Jackson workers live within a mile of their workplace and 35 percent live more than five miles (8 kilometers) away.

About 90 percent of Jackson workers, therefore, drive their own cars to work, and only 4 percent are able to walk to work.

Summary, Comparisons and Conclusions

The Jackson and Pskov samples were rather similar with regard to several personal background characteristics. There were slightly more women in Pskov (56 percent) than in Jackson (54 percent) and slightly more 18–24 year olds and 60–64 year olds in Jackson. Education distributions were also rather similar, although slightly more Jackson respondents had graduate school education than did those respondents in Pskov. Nonetheless, it is very difficult to make more than gross comparisons given the large differences in the education systems of the U.S. and the USSR.

More respondents in Jackson were married or were widowed, while more Pskov respondents had never been married. Proportions of divorced and separated people in the two cities were rather similar, about 10 to 15

Table 3.4
Employment Background of Jackson Respondents
(Totals may exceed 100% due to rounding)

	Jackson	Male	Female
(n=)	(724)	(320)	(404)
Employment Status			
Employed for pay	70	85	58
Retired	5	5	5
Disabled	2	2	2
Housewife	13	0	23
Maternity	2	1	3
Between jobs	4	3	4
Other	2	2	2
Student	4	3	5
	100%	100%	100%
EMPLOYED PERSONS:			
Branch of Economy			
(n=)	(474)	(255)	(219)
Manufacturing	26	34	16
Agriculture	0	0	0
Construction	3	4	1
Public transport	1	2	1
Other transport	3	6	1
Housing, utilities	6	9	3
Financial	2	0	4
Trade, retail	9	8	10
Food	6	5	7
Consumer	7	5	9
Health	8	1	16
Science	3	4	2
Culture, art	0	0	0
Education	8	6	12
Civic, gov't	3	4	2
Other	17	15	20
	100%	100%	100%
Workweek			
Six days	14	21	6
Five days	69	67	71
Four days	5	2	9
Other, varied	12	10	14
	100%	100%	100%

Table 3.4—continued

	Jackson	Male	Female
Shift			
One (day) shift	67	71	62
Two shifts	5	4	6
Three shifts	3	3	3
Varied	16	14	18
Other	10	9	11
	100%	100%	100%
Distance to work			
Less than 1 mile	12	12	12
1-2 miles	18	19	17
2-4 miles	15	17	12
4-5 miles	19	17	21
5-12 miles	23	22	25
More than 12 miles	12	14	13
	100%	100%	100%
Means of Transportation			
Walking	4	4	3
Bicycle	0	0	0
Moped	1	1	1
Car (own)	90	89	92
Public transport	*	0	1
Company	2	2	2
Other	4	5	2
	100%	100%	100%

percent. While the proportion with children in Jackson was slightly lower than in Pskov, most parents in Pskov had only one child; in Jackson, there were far more parents with three or more children.

About five respondents out of six (84 percent) in Pskov lived in a large apartment building. That was true for only 22 percent in Jackson, where two-thirds of the sample lived in single-family houses. Jackson residents also lived much further from work and from the center of the city than did Pskov residents. Again, the large differences in city planning, building construction and transportation systems make direct comparison of housing characteristics most difficult.

With regard to household appliances and technology, most Pskov families (95 percent) cooked with gas stoves, while in Jackson respondents used electric and gas stoves about equally. A far higher percentage of

Jackson households had microwave ovens than did those in Pskov. Refrigerators were almost universal in both cities. While more Jackson households had food processors, dishwashers and coffee machines, far more Pskov households had technology for canning and preserving food. The two sites were similar in ownership of washing machines, vacuum cleaners and sewing machines, however. More Jackson households had bicycles (for adults) and both two-wheeled and four-wheeled motor vehicles.

With regard to communications access, far more households in Jackson had telephones, color televisions and stereo equipment; however, roughly equivalent proportions had access to some television set and to large collections (over 100 volumes) of books in the two cities.

The two sites were also rather equivalent in access to home musical instruments. Americans had more pianos, more Soviets had accordions. About one in five respondents in both countries had access to a guitar. The same rough equivalence could be found for sports equipment. While slightly more Americans possessed collections of tools and cameras, more Soviets had access to checker or chess sets.

Employment

Here we come across significant differences in the population structure, with a higher proportion of both men and women in Pskov working than is the case in Jackson. More Jackson residents are housewives, unemployed or students. Large numbers of the Pskov workforce are in manufacturing, construction and transportation, while more Jackson workers are in service jobs—trades and retail, food, consumer services and health—and in services and education. Higher proportions of Pskov workers work five-day workweeks and single day shifts. Jackson workers live much further (more than twice as far as average) from work than do Pskov workers; henceforth, they must drive rather than walk to work.

Again, there are striking similarities between the two sites. Similarly, there are not any marked male-female differences found at either site, either in the structure of the workweek, the type of shift work, the distance to work or the means of transportation to commute to work.

The daily schedules of American and Soviet men were more likely to be similar than those of American and Soviet women. That was mainly because most women in the Soviet Union under the age of 65 have jobs. While 58 percent of women in Jackson were employed, some 80 percent of Pskov women were; the employment figures for men were 91 percent in Pskov and 85 percent in Jackson. These will be the main factors that affect the use of time by American and Soviet women as shown in the next chapter.

4

Time Use Patterns
in Pskov and in Jackson

The focus of this chapter centers on the *types* of time use respondents reported in their time diaries. These data are shown first for certain very broad categories of time use for the most basic population groups—such as employed men, employed women or housewives. More detailed breakdowns of the sample are then presented by factors such as age and education.

These more detailed tables employ a collapsed coding scheme from that shown in Chapter 2. That collapsed scheme is shown in Figure 4.1, which also shows the specific activities in Figure 2.2 that comprised each of these collapsed categories. They also show the four broadest categories into which time use is categorized: work (contracted time), housework and family care (committed time), personal care (necessary time) and free time (discretionary time). Two calculations of free time are shown, one conforming to the definition in Szalai et al. (1966) and the other to the definition used in Szalai et al. (1972). The main difference between the two is that the first includes certain child-care activities, helping behavior and rest as free time, while the second excludes these activities but instead includes travel-associated activities with free-time activities.

The latter tables in this chapter, then, review the many differences in how time is spent across the week in Pskov and in Jackson for different demographic groups. The twenty-seven categories of time use in Figure 4.1 are reviewed first for the important factor of employment status, separately for employed and non-employed men and for employed and non-employed women. The next set of calculations involves differences for men and women regarding the age factor. Education differences are examined in the third set of calculations. The fourth and final set of calculations involves differences between married and non-married men and women.

The reader will recognize that these bivariate tables capture only the broadest differences by these background factors. As in any bivariate analysis, many of the resulting Pskov-Jackson differences arise simply because in the two cities the various age, education and marital status groupings differ on other characteristics as well—most notably by employment status. Nonetheless, we shall find some surprising contrasting pat-

		<u>Pskov</u>	<u>Jackson</u>
1)	Regular work	00–03,05	00–04
2)	Second job	04	05
3)	Non-work	06–08	06–08
4)	Trip to work	09	09
	WORK (00–09)		
5)	Preparing food	10	10
6)	Cleaning house	11–12, 17	11–13
7)	Laundry	13–14	14–15
8)	Other housekeeping	15, 18	16, 19
9)	Gardening, pets	16, 17, 19	17
10)	Child care	20–24, 26, 28	20–22, 26, 27
11)	Shopping	30–31, 34–38	30, 31, 34–37
12)	Non-work trips	29, 39, 49, 59*,	29, 39, 49, 59*,
		69*, 79*, 89*, 99*	69*, 79*, 89*, 99*
	HOUSEWORK (10–19, 20–29, 30–39)		
13)	Sleep	45	45
14)	Personal care	32, 33, 40, 41, 47, 48	32, 33, 40, 41, 48
15)	Eating	43, 44	43, 44
16)	Rest	46, 98	47, 98
	PERSONAL CARE (40–49)		
17)	Education	50–58	50–56
18)	Organizations	60–68	60–68
19)	Radio	90	90
20)	Television	91	91
21)	Reading	93–95	93–95
22)	Social life	26, 28, 42, 75–78, 87	24, 42, 75–78, 87
23)	Conversation	25, 96	23, 56
24)	Walking	27, 82	25, 82
25)	Soprts	80–81	80–81
26)	Various leisure	83–86, 88, 92, 97	83–86, 88, 92, 97
27)	Spectacles	70–74, 77	70–74

FREE TIME #1 (23, 25, 46, 47, 50–58, 60–68, 70–78, 80–88, 90–98)
    (Szalai et al., 1966)
FREE TIME #2 (50–99)
    (Szalai et al., 1972)

*Included as part of free time in FREE TIME #2

Figure 4.1
Collapsed Activity Code for Analysis of Data
(Includes activities—See Figure 2.2)

terns in the two data sets despite large differences in sample composition in the two sites.

Thus, the most basic time-diary data from the Pskov 1986 study are reviewed in Tables 4.1 through 4.3 and the more detailed figures in Tables 4.4 through 4.7. (These data are weighted by day of the week and by sex and age for respondents aged 18–65 only.) The data are presented in hours per week to facilitate comparisons in these tables.

A main limitation of those data tables is that the figures are reported for all respondents, whether they engaged in the activity or not. This limitation of the data will be addressed in future analyses that will take into account important differences in the participation *rates* for these various activities.

Time Use in Pskov

The general time-use patterns of the employed and non-employed segments of the population in Pskov are shown in Table 4.1. As we can see, the employed population spends about a quarter of its weekly time (over

Table 4.1
General Differences in Time Use in Pskov in 1986
(in hours per week)

Types of activity	Employed		Students		Retired		Full-Time Home- makers	Total 18-65 Years	
	Men	Women	Men	Women	Men	Women	Women	Men	Women
(n=)	(797)	(1056)	(16)	(30)	(52)	(143)	(13)	(875)	(1306)
1.Work	43.5	40.0	37.7*	34.5*	0	0.1	0	39.9	32.3
2.Work-related	10.0	8.0	0	0	0	0	0	9.3	6.5
3.Housework	10.5	22.0	4.5	15.4	23.9	38.1	43.4	11.8	24.9
4.Personal Needs	64.8	66.4	75.1	73.8	70.0	75.4	75.0	65.8	67.5
5.Free time	34.5	26.5	39.2	35.4	59.1	46.6	45.2	37.1	31.3
6.Non-work trips	4.6	5.8	9.4	9.3	7.1	7.5	4.4	4.9	5.4
7.Other	0.1	0.1	2.1	0.4	0	0.3	0	0	0.1
Total	168	168	168	168	168	168	168	168	168

*Study, paid work and related types of activities of students are listed as work activities.

Table 4.2
Distribution of Time on Housework and Family in Pskov in 1986
(in hours per week)

Types of activity	Employed Men	Employed Women
1. Work in the household including:	7.1	16.0
Preparing food	2.5	7.6
Cleaning the house	4.0	4.7
Washing and ironing	0.3	3.6
Gardening	0.3	0.1
2. Care and upbringing of children	1.6	3.1
3. Shopping	1.8	2.9
TOTAL	10.5	22.0

40 hours) on various forms of production activities, including extra and overtime work. An additional six to ten hours per week is spent on work-related activities, such as commuting to work, changing clothes at the workplace, and the like.

It can be seen in Table 4.1 that working women spend twice as much time on household chores (22.0 hours per week) than employed men (10.5 hours per week). Table 4.2 shows in more detail that almost three-fourths of the total time spent on such activities as cooking, cleaning, child care, repair and upkeep of clothes and laundry is attributed to the working women in Pskov. Table 4.2 also shows that child care consumes 3.1 hours per week of an employed woman's time, and that shopping and obtaining various household services require 2.9 hours. While men spend much less time on housework than women, the time that they do spend on such activity is directed primarily to cleaning house, shopping and gardening.

Thus, employed men spend 10.5 hours per week on household activities, while employed women spend 22 hours. Physiological needs take about 65–66 hours. About five hours is spent on travel activities not related to work. This leaves employed men with 34.5 hours of free time per week and employed women with 26.5 hours.

In contrast, the time use patterns of the non-employed population is quite different. Students spend 35–38 hours per week on education and related activities. Not surprisingly, they spend less time on household activities and have more free time. Unlike the situation for employed men and women, male and female students have about the same amount of free time.

The time-use pattern of pensioners, disabled people and housewives is very much the same. They spend more time than employed people on household activities—24 hours per week for men and 38 hours for women. They also have much more free time; male pensioners and disabled men have about 59 hours of free time per week, while women in these categories have about 47 hours of free time per week.

Considering that 85 percent of the urban population in Pskov aged 18 to 65 works at various enterprises and state institutions, that is obviously the dominating factor in the city in defining the time-use patterns of the population. With different proportions of non-employed groups in the city population and in various age, family status etc., groups, there is some distortion in the average time usage as calculated for all respondents. Therefore, Tables 4.4 to 4.7 present the breakdown of data for the employed population on these socio-demographic factors.

Table 4.3 shows that the amount of free time and its usage is also different for working men and women. Working men have 34.5 hours of free time per week, while working women have only 26.5 hours of free time each week. Mass media (radio, TV and reading) occupy from 54 percent to 59 percent of the time available, the bulk of which is spent watching TV, with employed people spending 1.5–2 hours per day with TV.

Sport and active home recreation activities also occupy considerable amounts of the employed population's free time (12–14 percent); however, the absolute quantity of time spent on sport is relatively small. Thus, each week women spend only 0.6 hours on sport and outdoor recreation activities while men spend about two hours.

Significant portions of free time are spent on social interaction and relaxation. Less than 3 percent of free time is spent on cultural institutions, such as attending movies. Likewise, relatively small amounts of time are spent on education and civic activity.

In summary, the use of free time by the working population in Pskov is rather diversified. As a result of television, free time is spent mostly at home. The passive nature of such uses of free time means that people are more likely to be spectators than "actors" or active personalities.

This pattern of free-time usage is also, of course, affected by the work conditions, everyday activities, recreation, industrialization, and urbanization processes in the larger society. We turn first to the factor of employment status.

Table 4.3
1986 Pskov Free Time Differences by Gender
(in Hours Per Week)

	Employed Men	Employed Women
Education	0.7	0.8
Organizations	1.2	0.7
Spectacles	0.9	0.6
Sports and recreation	4.1	4.3
Walking	1.5	1.4
Sports	1.8	0.6
Hobby	0.8	2.3
Various leisure:	27.7	20.1
Radio	0.2	0.1
Television	14.5	10.7
Reading	5.8	3.5
Social Life	2.6	2.1
Conversation	1.2	1.3
Resting (passive)	<u>3.4</u>	<u>2.4</u>
Total Free Time	34.5 Hours	26.5 Hours

Employment Status

Table 4.4 indicates the effects status and sex differences have on the use of time among employed people. It is natural that those who are not employed have no work-related time expenditures, but different types of non-employed groups (students, pensioners, invalids, housewives) do have quite distinct time-use patterns as shown in Table 4.1. Therefore, this needs to be considered in the analysis of time use by the non-employed population shown in Table 4.4.

Age

Age-related differences in the use of time by the working population in Pskov are shown in Table 4.5. As we see, people in the 25–49 age group spend more time on work and related activities than those who are 18–24 years old or 50 and above. However, these differences are not very signifi-

Table 4.4
1986 Pskov Time Use Data by Sex and Employment Status
(in hours per week; weighted by day of the week, age and sex)

	Men			Women			Total
n=	Not Emp. (75)	Emp. (797)	Total (875)	Not Emp. (250)	Emp. (1056)	Total (1306)	Sample (2181)
1) Regular work	5.0	43.4	39.8	0.4	39.9	32.2	35.5
2) Second job	0	0.1	0.1	0.1	0.2	0.2	0.1
3) Non work	0.9	4.8	4.4	0.4	3.9	3.2	3.7
4) Trip to work	1.0	5.2	4.8	0.1	4.2	3.4	4.0
Work Related	7.0	53.5	49.2	1.0	48.0	38.8	43.3
5) Preparing food	3.9	2.5	2.7	10.5	7.6	8.2	5.8
6) Cleaning house	2.6	1.4	1.5	6.9	3.9	4.5	3.2
7) Laundry	0.9	0.3	0.3	5.0	3.6	3.8	2.3
8) Other housekeeping	4.5	2.6	2.8	1.6	0.8	0.9	1.7
9) Gardening, pets	0.8	0.3	0.4	0.3	0.1	0.2	0.3
Housework	12.7	7.2	7.7	24.2	16.0	17.6	13.3
10) Child care	1.1	1.6	1.5	9.2	3.2	4.4	3.1
11) Shopping	2.1	1.8	1.8	3.4	2.9	3.0	2.5
12) Non-work trips	7.4	4.6	4.9	7.0	5.0	5.4	5.2
Family Tasks	10.6	7.9	8.2	19.6	11.1	12.7	10.8
13) Sleep	59.5	53.5	54.1	58.0	54.6	55.3	54.8
14) Personal Care	7.9	6.0	6.2	6.4	6.6	6.6	6.4
15) Eating	7.6	5.3	5.5	7.6	5.2	5.7	5.6
Personal Needs	75.4	64.8	65.8	72.1	66.4	67.5	66.8
16) Education	13.3	0.7	1.9	8.2	0.8	2.2	2.1
17) Organizations	0.6	1.2	1.1	0.6	0.7	0.7	0.9
18) Radio	0.6	0.2	0.3	0.1	0.1	0.1	0.2
19) Television	15.9	14.5	14.6	13.6	10.7	11.2	12.7
20) Reading	9.8	5.8	6.1	6.1	3.5	4.0	5.0
21) Social life	3.8	2.6	2.7	4.0	2.1	2.5	2.6
22) Conversation	2.0	1.2	1.3	2.3	1.3	1.5	1.4
23) Walking	4.1	1.5	1.7	4.2	1.4	1.9	1.5
24) Sports	1.5	1.8	1.8	0.3	0.6	0.5	1.1
25) Various leisure	2.3	0.8	0.9	5.7	2.3	2.9	2.1
26) Spectacles	2.6	0.9	1.1	0.6	0.6	0.6	0.8
27) Resting	6.1	3.4	5.4	5.4	2.4	3.0	3.3
Total Free Time #1	62.3	34.5	37.1	51.0	26.5	31.3	33.5
28) Free Time #2	63.3	34.0	36.8	46.5	25.7	29.8	32.8
29) Total Time	168	168	168	168	168	168	168

Table 4.5
1986 Pskov Time Use Differences by Sex and Age (in hours per week; weighted by day of the week, age and sex)

| | Men | | | | | | Women | | | | | | Total |
	18-24	25-29	30-39	40-49	50-59	60-65	18-24	25-29	30-39	40-49	50-59	60-65	Sample
1) Regular work	35.2	46.8	45.6	41.3	41.9	36.5	39.5	41.8	38.2	41.9	40.2	33.3	41.5
2) Second job	0.1	0.2	0	0	0	0	0.1	0.2	0.2	0.2	0.2	0	0.1
3) Non work	3.8	4.9	5.1	4.8	4.7	4.5	4.3	3.9	3.5	4.1	3.8	2.8	7.3
4) Trip to work	4.7	5.4	5.3	5.6	5.0	4.3	4.1	3.9	4.0	3.9	4.4	3.6	4.2
Work Related	43.9	57.4	56.8	51.7	51.7	45.1	48.0	49.8	45.4	50.5	48.7	39.7	50.6
5) Preparing food	1.7	2.2	2.7	2.5	2.6	2.8	5.0	6.0	8.8	8.6	8.7	8.4	5.3
6) Cleaning house	1.9	0.9	1.4	1.5	1.5	1.5	2.8	3.0	4.1	4.6	4.5	4.7	2.7
7) Laundry	0.3	0.3	0.3	0.1	0.4	0.3	2.4	2.9	4.4	4.3	2.9	4.7	2.0
8) Other housekeeping	2.2	1.5	2.8	3.3	2.9	3.0	0.8	0.5	0.8	0.7	1.0	1.2	1.6
9) Gardening, pets	0.3	0.2	0.3	0.5	0.4	0.2	0	0	0.2	0.4	0.3	0.2	0.2
Housework	6.3	5.1	7.5	8.3	7.8	7.6	11.0	12.4	18.1	18.4	17.4	19.1	11.9
10) Child care	1.7	1.9	2.7	0.9	0.4	2.0	2.3	5.8	5.0	1.8	0.3	0.6	2.4
11) Shopping	1.7	1.2	2.0	1.7	2.3	2.5	2.3	2.3	2.9	3.6	2.9	4.0	2.4
12) Non-work trips	6.1	4.5	4.6	3.8	3.9	4.7	6.0	5.6	4.9	4.2	4.7	4.5	4.8
Family Tasks	9.4	7.6	9.3	6.4	6.6	9.3	10.5	13.7	12.8	9.5	7.9	9.0	9.6
13) Sleep	55.5	53.3	53.7	52.9	52.8	54.7	56.0	55.1	53.6	54.0	54.6	56.3	54.1
14) Personal care	6.1	6.0	5.7	6.2	6.1	7.6	7.8	6.5	6.4	6.3	6.4	6.5	6.4
15) Eating	5.0	5.0	5.2	5.3	5.7	6.4	4.7	5.1	5.3	5.4	5.1	6.2	5.3
Personal Needs	66.1	64.4	64.7	64.4	64.7	68.7	68.4	66.6	65.4	65.7	66.1	68.5	65.7

16) Education	0.2	1.9	0.4	0.9	0.2	0	1.6	1.0	1.1	0.2	0.2	0.8	0.8
17) Organization	0.7	1.1	1.2	1.2	1.4	1.7	0.3	0.8	0.8	0.6	1.2	0.6	0.7
18) Radio	0.1	0.1	0.2	0.3	0.3	0.8	0	0	0	0	0.1	0.1	0.1
19) Television	14.5	12.7	14.4	14.9	15.7	16.2	10.5	10.1	10.1	10.7	11.5	12.4	12.4
20) Reading	5.5	6.1	4.8	6.2	6.6	6.5	3.7	3.1	3.7	3.1	3.3	6.1	4.6
21) Social life	5.0	3.3	2.3	1.6	2.3	0.4	3.2	2.5	1.9	1.6	1.9	1.5	2.3
22) Conversation	1.2	1.2	1.1	1.2	1.4	0.7	3.7	3.1	3.7	3.1	3.3	6.1	4.6
23) Walking	3.3	1.1	1.3	1.2	1.3	1.6	1.8	1.3	1.5	0.9	1.2	2.0	1.4
24) Sports	2.0	1.9	1.1	2.0	1.6	5.8	0.8	0.4	0.7	0.5	0.5	0.5	1.2
25) Various leisure	2.3	0.5	0.4	1.0	0.8	0.1	3.3	1.4	2.0	0.2	0.5	2.6	1.6
26) Spectacles	4.1	1.2	0.5	0.4	0.3	0.3	1.4	1.0	0.4	0.4	0.3	2.0	0.8
27) Resting	3.5	2.4	2.8	3.5	5.4	3.3	1.8	2.4	2.2	2.5	3.2	4.4	2.4
Total Free Time #1	42.3	33.5	30.4	34.3	37.3	37.3	32.1	25.5	25.8	23.7	27.5	39.1	30.2
28) Free Time #2	44.4	32.2	29.1	33.9	36.4	41.1	31.6	23.5	24.0	23.8	26.8	29.6	29.6
29) Total Time	168	168	168	168	168	168	168	168	168	168	168	168	168

cant due to the 41 hour norm of working time per week established in the USSR. Some differences are determined by different duration of work shifts, time spent commuting to work, and other factors related to work.

Significant differences are found in time expenditures of women, especially on housework which tends to increase with age. While men aged 18–29 spend 11–12 hours per week, those aged 30–39 spend more than 18 hours. Time spent on child care also differs with age. Men and women aged 25–39 spend the most amount of time on child care since these are the peak child-rearing years.

Night sleep duration is about the same for all age groups in the working population of Pskov. It is slightly higher for those aged 18–24 and for those aged 60–65. Those aged 25–49 have less free time as compared to those younger and older than themselves.

Men aged 25–29 and women aged 18–24 years spend more of their free time on education than do those in other groups. Civic activities tend to occupy more time as one's age increases.

Men aged 60 and above spend some time listening to radio as a primary activity. All age groups spend much of their free time watching TV, but people aged 50 and above devote more time to the set. Those aged 60–65 tend to spend most of their time reading.

Social interaction tends to be higher among those under 30. On the other hand, conversation time is much more constant with age. Time spent in outdoor recreation and sports tends to be higher among the very young and the very old for men, but not for women. Hobby and other leisure activities are higher among older women, but not among older men.

The major patterns by age are found at the extremes. Adults under age 30 and over 60 tend to work less, sleep more and have more free time than middle-age groups. In addition, young adults do less housework, take more education courses, get less involved in public activity and spend more time socializing than those in older age groups.

Education

Time-use differences by education are shown in Table 4.6. It can be seen that there is no clear correlation between time spent working and the level of education a person has achieved. Women at the various education levels spend about the same amount of time on housework (about 26–27 hours per week). Less educated men spend less time on housework (13 hours a week); women with secondary and higher education spend 14–16 hours per week. Similarly, no notable differences in time spent on physiological needs can be found among various education groups.

Men with secondary and higher education have a bit more free time than less educated people. Women with higher education are also found to have more free time, with the notable exception of women with only 4–6 years of education. Women with the least amount of education report more free time than women with higher levels of education. These education differences also reflect differences in the types of free-time activities; for example, better educated people devote more time to education, public activities and reading, but less time to watching television.

Marital Status

The differences by marital status shown in Table 4.7 are rather significant. Married men spend more time at work; however, married and non-married women spend about the same amount of time at work. Married working men spend almost the same amount of time doing housework as do non-married men, while married women spend almost five more hours per week doing housework than do the non-married women.

Married men and women spend about two hours more per week sleeping than do non-married men and women. They spend about the same amount of time in personal care and eating as non-married people.

Married men and women, of course, spend more time in child-care activities; they also spend more time shopping. Non-married people spend more time in non-work travel than married people.

Non-married men have 9–12 hours more of free time per week than married men, while non-married women have 4–6 hours more free time per week than married women. Non-married people spend more of their free time on adult education and in social life, hobbies, and visiting cultural/recreational institutions. Married men (but not married women) spend more time in civic activities and less time walking outdoors. Non-married women also spend more of their free time reading. Television viewing is only slightly lower among the non-married. Non-married people spend more time in certain out-of-home activities, particularly in adult education, socializing and attending entertainment and cultural events; they can also afford to spend more time sleeping.

Time Use in Jackson

The basic time-diary data from the 1986 Jackson study are shown in Tables 4.8–4.10 and the more detailed and complete tabulations in Tables 4.11–4.14. These tables exclude about ninety other respondents who had more than 100 minutes of missing time data across the day; in that way, the missing data times were made equivalent to those encountered in the 1965 study. Again, the data are presented in average hours of time per week for all respondents, whether respondents engaged in the activity or not.

Table 4.6
1986 Pskov Time Use Differences by Sex and Education
(in hours per week; weighted by day of the week, age and sex)

Grades n=	Men					Women				
	4-6 (64)	7-9 (155)	10-11 (266)	Tech (177)	College (126)	4-6 (65)	7-9 (157)	10-11 (267)	Tech (365)	College (198)
1) Regular work	45.2	41.8	44.4	42.1	43.7	34.4	40.7	42.1	39.0	39.2
2) Second job	0	0.1	0	0.1	0.3	0.5	0	0.2	0.2	0
3) Non work	5.1	4.7	5.1	4.4	4.2	3.2	4.2	4.0	4.0	3.5
4) Trip to work	5.8	5.2	5.0	5.5	5.0	3.6	4.2	4.2	4.3	4.0
Work Related	56.1	51.8	54.6	52.2	53.2	41.6	49.1	50.4	47.4	46.7
5) Preparing food	3.2	2.6	2.4	2.6	2.1	8.4	8.3	7.3	7.7	7.2
6) Cleaning house	1.2	1.7	1.5	1.1	1.5	5.2	4.2	3.4	3.9	3.8
7) Laundry	0.3	0.4	0.3	0.1	0.3	3.2	4.0	3.8	3.4	3.4
8) Other housekeeping	3.4	3.2	2.6	2.4	2.0	1.1	1.2	0.8	0.6	0.6
9) Gardening, pets	0.3	0.5	0.2	0.3	0.4	0.4	0.2	0	0.1	0.2
Housework	8.3	8.4	7.1	6.5	6.3	18.2	17.9	15.5	15.7	15.2
10) Child care	0.3	1.1	2.0	1.3	2.2	0.7	1.9	3.9	3.2	3.8
11) Shopping	1.3	2.0	1.0	2.0	1.3	2.8	3.3	2.8	3.0	2.6
12) Non-work trips	3.1	4.3	4.7	5.2	4.6	5.2	4.9	4.8	5.2	5.1
Family Tasks	4.8	7.4	8.5	8.5	8.1	8.6	10.1	11.4	11.4	11.4

13) Sleep	53.6	54.8	53.2	53.1	53.3	56.0	55.0	53.6	55.2	54.3
14) Personal care	6.0	6.5	5.8	5.9	6.4	6.3	6.3	6.8	6.6	6.6
15) Eating	5.4	5.8	5.1	5.3	5.5	6.2	5.2	5.1	5.0	5.2
Personal Needs	65.0	67.0	64.7	64.3	65.2	68.3	66.4	65.5	66.8	66.1
16) Education	0	0.1	0.4	1.6	1.1	0.3	0.3	1.0	1.1	0.5
17) Organizations	0.8	0.1	0.8	1.9	2.2	1.0	0.7	0.4	0.4	1.7
18) Radio	0.1	0.4	0.3	0.2	0.2	0.2	0	0	0.1	0.1
19) Television	17.5	16.2	14.7	13.6	11.9	13.7	10.7	10.8	10.5	9.7
20) Reading	3.8	6.0	5.3	6.5	6.3	2.6	3.0	3.2	3.3	4.8
21) Social life	2.8	1.4	2.7	2.6	3.3	1.1	2.4	1.5	2.5	2.5
22) Conversation	1.8	1.3	1.0	1.2	1.3	2.5	0.8	1.3	1.2	1.7
23) Walking	1.1	1.1	1.6	1.7	1.5	1.7	0.9	1.5	1.4	1.4
24) Sports	1.2	0.9	1.5	2.2	3.1	0.1	0.3	0.6	0.5	1.0
25) Various leisure	0.6	0.3	0.7	1.0	1.4	3.2	1.7	1.9	2.6	2.4
26) Spectacles	0.6	0.2	1.4	1.4	0.3	0	0.6	0.7	0.7	0.6
27) Resting	3.8	5.4	3.1	2.8	2.7	4.7	3.2	2.1	2.2	2.0
Total Free Time #1	33.9	33.4	33.7	36.6	35.2	31.0	24.5	25.1	26.6	28.2
Free Time #2	33.4	31.7	33.5	36.9	34.4	30.4	24.7	24.1	26.1	26.7
Total Time	168	168	168	168	168	168	168	168	168	168

Table 4.7
1986 Pskov Time Use Differences by Sex and Marital Status
(in hours per week; weighted by day of the week, age and sex)

	MEN		WOMEN	
	Married	Non-Married	Married	Non-Married
n=	(682)	(113)	(697)	(356)
1) Regular work	45.1	39.7	39.8	39.9
2) Second job	0	0.3	0.2	0.2
3) Non work	5.0	5.8	3.8	4.0
4) Trip to work	5.4	4.3	4.1	4.3
Work Related	55.5	50.1	47.8	48.3
5) Preparing food	2.4	3.4	8.7	5.8
6) Cleaning house	1.5	1.1	4.2	3.2
7) Laundry	0.3	0.1	3.9	2.9
8) Other housekeeping	2.7	2.4	0.7	0.9
9) Gardening, pets	0.3	0.1	0.2	0.1
Housework	7.2	7.1	17.7	13.0
10) Child care	1.8	0.3	4.1	1.6
11) Shopping	1.8	1.7	3.1	2.4
12) Non-work trips	4.2	6.6	4.9	5.2
Family Tasks	7.8	8.7	12.1	9.2
13) Sleep	53.1	54.9	54.7	56.1
14) Personal care	6.1	5.8	6.5	6.9
15) Eating	5.3	5.4	5.3	5.1
Personal Needs	64.5	66.3	66.5	68.1
16) Education	0.6	1.1	0.5	1.4
17) Organizations	1.2	0.9	0.7	0.8
18) Radio	0.2	0.3	0	0.1
19) Television	14.5	14.1	10.9	10.3
20) Reading	5.7	5.9	3.2	3.9
21) Social life	2.3	3.7	1.9	2.5
22) Conversation	1.1	1.6	1.3	1.3
23) Walking	1.2	2.8	1.3	1.5
24) Sports	1.6	2.8	0.5	0.8
25) Various leisure	0.7	1.3	1.9	2.9
26) Spectacles	0.5	3.5	0.3	1.3
27) Resting	3.3	3.9	2.3	2.5
Free Time #1	33.0	41.8	24.9	29.3
28) Free Time #2	32.0	44.2	23.5	29.7
29) Total Time	168	168	168	168

Table 4.8
General Differences in Time Use in Jackson
(in hours per week)

	Employed		Non-Employed		TOTAL	
	Men	Women	Men	Women	Men	Women
Work	41.8	35.3	3.4	1.5	35.6	20.8
Work-related	6.4	5.5	.9	.1	5.5	3.2
Housework	10.7	17.5	17.1	34.6	12.0	24.6
Personal Needs	66.2	67.7	73.8	72.8	67.3	69.5
Free time	36.7	34.6	65.3	51.7	41.3	42.3
Non-work trips	6.1	7.3	7.9	7.5	6.4	7.3
TOTAL	168	168	168	168	168	168

General Time Use Differences

As shown in Table 4.8, work time consumes about 17 percent of the total time of Jackson residents, moreso for men than for women. This includes work commute time of about four hours a week for employed men and three hours for employed women.

Housework hours average about 7 percent of the total time for Jackson men and closer to 15 percent of the time for Jackson women; these figures are half again as high among non-working men and women as among those who are employed.

Table 4.9 presents a closer look at time spent on housework by respondents in Jackson. In general, employed women do 65 percent more housework than employed men. Regarding cooking, laundry and child care, the ratios are more than two to one. Shopping times are high among women as well. Men do more "other" housework—yard work and repairs—however.

Personal care (shown in Table 4.8) consumes about 40 percent of all time during the week for both men and women. Most of that time is for sleep. Men average about two hours less personal care time than do women, whether employed or not employed. Employed people have 5–7 hours less personal-care time than do non-employed people.

Free time is half again as high among non-employed as among employed women and more than 75 percent higher among non-employed men. Overall, however, both sexes average about 25 percent free time across the week—closer to 20 percent among employed people.

Table 4.9
Distribution of Time on Housework and Family in Jackson
(in hours per week)

Types of activity	Employed Men	Employed Women	Total Sample
1. Work in the household including:	7.6	11.3	13.1
Preparing food	1.7	4.1	4.0
Washing and ironing	5.6	1.5	1.3
Cleaning the house	2.2	4.4	5.0
Other	3.1	1.3	2.8
2. Care and upbringing of children	.8	2.0	2.0
3. Shopping	2.3	4.2	3.4
Total	10.7 hrs.	17.5 hrs.	18.5 hrs.

A detailed breakdown of this free time is shown in Table 4.10. Here it can be seen that more than half of free time is spent on the mass media, with television consuming 44 percent of the free time of men and 39 percent of the free time of women.

Social life is the second most popular way of spending free time, being somewhat higher among women than among men. Sports and outdoor recreation comprise the third most time-consuming type of leisure activities.

Employment Status

Table 4.11 presents the basic breakdown of the sample by sex and by employment status. It can be seen that this breakdown highlights how time spent at work impacts the time usage of both men and women. Thus, employed men average almost six hours of work per day (41.8 hours across the entire week) and employed women average more than five hours of work each day as well (35.3 hours per week).

This work time has a very large impact on other daily activities, as do commuting times (3.5 hours for men and 2.9 hours for women), other activities at work (2.6 hours for men and 2.4 hours for women) and second jobs. In total, their employment consumes more than 48 hours a week of employed hours a week of employed men's time and 40 hours of employed women's time. Work-related activities (which include unemployment activities, part-time jobs and "odd jobs") take up less than six hours a week of the time of both non-employed men and women.

These work hours have considerable impact on the time spent on housework by employed men and women. Employed men spend only about an hour per day (7.6 hours per week) on housework activities compared to nearly two hours (13.6 weekly hours) for non-employed men. The gap is much larger between employed women (10.3 hours per week) and non-employed women (25 hours per week.) On all housework activities except laundry, employed women spend less than half as much time as do non-employed women; the gap for laundry is also quite large (2.6 hours for non-employed women as compared to 1.5 hours for employed women).

Employed people also spend less time on personal-care activities. This includes time spent for sleeping (1 to 4 hours less), personal care (.2 to .6

Table 4.10
1986 Jackson Free Time Differences by Gender
(in Hours Per Week)

	Employed Men	Employed Women
Education	0.9	1.6
Organizations	1.7	2.3
Spectacles	0.3	0.6
Sports and recreation	3.7	2.8
Walking	0.6	0.1
Sports	2.1	1.4
Hobby	1.0	1.3
Various leisure:	30.0	27.0
Radio	0.6	.3
Television	16.1	13.6
Reading	2.9	3.1
Social Life	6.4	6.2
Conversation	1.9	2.4
Resting (passive)	2.1	1.4
Total Free Time	36.7 Hours	34.6 Hours

Table 4.11
1986 Jackson Time Use Differences by Sex and Employment Status
(in hours per week)

| | MEN | | | WOMEN | | | TOTAL |
| | Not Emp. | Employ | Total | Not Emp. | Employ | Total | SAMPLE |
n=	(48)	(252)	(301)	(141)	(188)	(329)	(630)
1) Regular work	3.4	41.8	35.6	1.5	35.3	20.8	27.9
2) Second job	0.0	0.3	0.3	0.0	0.0	0.1	0.1
3) Non work	0.2	2.6	2.2	0.0	2.4	1.4	1.9
4) Trip to work	0.7	3.5	3.0	0.1	2.9	1.7	2.3
Work Related	4.3	48.2	41.2	1.6	40.0	24.6	31.5
5) Preparing food	2.2	1.7	1.7	8.5	4.1	5.9	4.0
6) Cleaning house	6.8	2.2	3.0	10.3	4.4	6.9	5.0
7) Laundry	0.0	0.6	0.5	2.6	1.5	2.0	1.3
8) Other house- keeping	4.2	2.7	3.0	2.8	1.0	1.7	2.3
9) Gardening, pets	0.3	0.2	0.2	0.8	0.3	0.6	0.5
Housework	13.6	7.6	8.5	25.0	11.3	17.1	13.1
10) Child care	1.2	0.8	0.8	4.7	2.0	3.1	2.0
11) Shopping	2.3	2.3	2.3	4.9	4.2	4.4	3.4
12) Non-work trips	7.9	6.1	6.4	7.5	7.3	7.3	6.9
Family Tasks	11.4	9.2	9.6	16.9	13.5	14.8	12.4
13) Sleep	56.9	52.6	53.2	53.9	52.7	52.9	53.9
14) Personal care	7.3	7.1	7.1	9.7	9.1	9.3	8.3
15) Eating	9.6	6.5	7.0	9.1	5.9	7.3	7.1
Personal Needs	73.8	66.2	67.3	72.8	67.7	69.5	69.3
16) Education	6.6	0.9	1.9	4.0	1.6	2.6	2.2
17) Organiza- tions	1.7	1.7	1.7	2.0	2.3	2.2	2.0
18) Radio	1.4	0.6	0.7	0.2	0.3	0.1	0.4
19) Television	29.7	16.1	18.3	20.3	13.6	16.9	17.4
20) Reading	4.1	2.9	3.0	3.3	3.1	3.3	3.1
21) Social life	11.4	6.4	7.2	10.5	6.2	8.0	7.6
22) Conversa- tion	1.7	1.9	1.9	3.6	2.4	2.9	2.4
23) Walking	2.1	0.6	0.8	0.3	0.1	0.0	0.5
24) Sports	1.9	2.1	2.1	1.3	1.4	1.4	1.7

Table 4.11—continued

	MEN			WOMEN			TOTAL
n=	Not Emp. (48)	Employ (252)	Total (301)	Not Emp. (141)	Employ (188)	Total (329)	SAMPLE (630)
25) Various leisure	2.0	1.0	1.2	2.9	1.3	2.0	1.6
26) Spectacles	0.1	0.3	0.3	0.7	0.6	0.7	0.5
27) Resting	2.6	2.1	2.2	2.6	1.4	2.1	2.1
Free Time #1	65.3	36.7	41.3	51.7	34.6	42.3	41.6
Free Time #2	67.2	36.4	41.4	48.9	35.0	40.9	41.2
Total Time	168	168	168	168	168	168	168

hours less), eating at home or in restaurants (3 hours or less, although meals at work are included under work and need to be considered here), and resting (0.5 to 1.2 hours less).

Employed women also spend much less time in child care, probably again because they have fewer children. They also spend 0.7 hours less per week shopping. Time spent on non-work trips, however, is almost the same for employed and non-employed women. Employed men, on the other hand, spend much less time (1.8 hours per week) on non-work trips than do non-employed men.

It is in their free time that the employed differ most from their non-employed counterparts. Employed men have only 56 percent as much free time per week as do non-employed men, and employed women only 67 percent as much free time as non-employed women. That translates to almost 30 hours less free time per week for employed men and 14–17 hours less free time per week for employed women.

These differences come from a variety of free-time activities. It does come about proportionately from television, the main consumer of free-time activity for both men and women; this also tends to be the case for social life, hobby and adult education activities.

However, for many other free-time activities, the "trade-offs" involved do vary by sex and by employment status. Thus, employed men and women spend as much of their (lesser) free time as their non-employed counterparts in organizational activities, in reading, in sports activities and in attending spectacles and entertainment; they also spend proportionately less time listening to the radio and walking than do their non-employed counterparts. There are gender differences as well. Employed men do not show reduced conversation as do employed women, and they show much more difference in adult education activities.

Table 4.12
1985 Jackson Time Use Differences by Sex and Age
(in hours per week; weighted by day of the week, age and sex)

	Men						Women						Total
	18-24	25-29	30-39	40-49	50-59	60-65	18-24	25-29	30-39	40-49	50-59	60-65	Sample
n=	(66)	(42)	(66)	(51)	(48)	(28)	(71)	(45)	(68)	(56)	(50)	(34)	(630)
1) Regular work	34.9	34.3	39.3	35.0	42.1	19.9	18.4	21.2	25.7	22.5	21.8	12.5	27.9
2) Second job	1.0	0.0	0.1	0.2	0.0	0.0	0.0	0.0	0.0	0.0	0.2	0.0	0.1
3) Non work	1.6	2.0	2.9	2.8	2.3	1.3	1.7	1.5	1.4	2.1	0.9	0.5	1.9
4) Trip to work	2.4	2.8	3.0	2.8	4.2	1.4	1.6	1.6	2.2	1.9	1.7	0.6	2.3
Work Related	39.9	39.0	46.3	40.8	48.6	22.6	21.8	24.5	29.4	26.6	24.7	13.5	32.2
5) Preparing food	1.0	2.2	2.3	1.3	2.1	2.2	3.1	5.8	5.4	7.5	7.2	7.9	4.0
6) Cleaning house	2.8	2.2	2.3	1.5	3.1	8.5	4.7	7.5	7.1	7.0	7.6	8.7	5.0
7) Laundry	0.3	0.1	0.7	0.8	0.7	0.0	1.3	1.7	2.4	2.2	2.1	2.3	1.3
8) Other housekeeping	1.2	6.5	2.8	2.6	2.6	3.8	0.2	0.5	1.4	1.6	3.6	4.7	2.3
9) Gardening, pets	0.0	0.2	0.2	0.5	0.5	0.5	0.3	0.6	0.3	0.3	1.0	0.8	0.5
Housework	5.4	11.3	8.4	6.6	9.0	15.0	9.8	15.9	17.1	18.5	21.6	24.6	13.1
10) Child care	0.9	1.3	1.3	0.7	0.5	0.1	2.1	8.0	4.5	2.6	0.9	0.5	2.0
11) Shopping	1.4	1.7	2.1	3.1	3.6	1.9	4.5	4.2	4.0	5.6	4.1	4.2	3.4
12) Non-work trips	7.6	6.3	6.1	7.0	5.6	5.1	8.6	6.9	7.6	8.2	4.9	7.5	6.9
Family Tasks	9.9	9.4	9.3	10.8	9.7	7.2	15.3	19.2	16.1	16.3	9.9	12.1	12.4

13) Sleep	51.9	51.9	52.5	51.2	49.6	54.9	57.6	55.3	51.8	51.6	57.5	48.9	53.2
14) Personal care	5.9	7.5	7.8	7.2	7.6	7.3	9.0	9.2	8.6	9.3	10.8	10.8	8.3
15) Eating	4.8	5.1	7.0	7.5	8.6	11.4	6.2	6.3	6.2	7.5	8.9	10.5	7.1
Personal Needs	62.6	64.4	67.3	65.9	65.8	73.6	72.8	70.8	66.6	68.4	77.2	70.2	68.6
16) Education	5.2	2.4	1.3	0.0	0.2	0.3	8.2	0.7	0.6	3.1	0.9	0.0	2.2
17) Organizations	0.8	1.3	1.2	2.7	2.8	2.4	0.9	0.6	2.0	3.6	3.3	3.5	2.0
18) Radio	0.3	0.3	0.6	0.6	1.6	1.0	0.3	0.2	0.1	0.1	0.1	0.0	0.3
19) Television	19.6	19.5	16.4	18.9	14.2	23.8	18.5	15.4	13.4	11.9	21.0	20.1	17.4
20) Reading	1.7	2.7	2.7	3.4	3.6	6.4	2.3	1.5	3.3	4.4	4.3	3.8	3.1
21) Social life	9.6	5.5	7.2	9.0	4.1	6.2	9.4	9.7	8.6	5.6	4.4	10.4	7.6
22) Conversation	1.5	2.3	1.6	2.6	1.9	1.4	2.1	2.8	3.4	3.5	2.4	3.6	2.4
23) Walking	0.7	1.4	0.5	0.7	0.5	1.4	0.1	0.3	0.2	0.1	0.2	0.0	0.5
24) Sports	2.4	4.7	2.0	1.4	0.0	2.1	0.8	2.1	2.1	0.9	0.7	1.9	1.7
25) Various leisure	0.5	0.8	1.0	1.0	2.1	2.0	1.7	0.6	2.3	2.3	1.7	3.0	1.6
26) Spectacles	0.3	0.2	0.6	0.6	0.0	0.2	2.0	0.3	0.8	0.1	0.0	0.0	0.5
27) Resting	0.8	2.3	1.6	2.8	3.8	2.0	2.0	3.8	2.1	2.3	1.9	1.3	2.1
Free Time #1	43.9	43.7	36.9	43.6	34.9	49.3	48.4	37.6	38.8	38.1	40.9	47.7	41.6
Free Time #2	46.1	44.3	37.0	41.6	32.4	50.7	48.4	35.9	37.3	37.1	40.1	45.5	41.2
Total Time	168	168	168	168	168	168	68	168	168	168	168	168	168

Thus, it is mainly in the area of free time activities that employed men and women subtract the more than 40 hours more time they devote to work than do non-employed men and women. One also finds decreased time spent in most housework activities, and to a much lesser extent in personal care activities. But the main difference found is that employed men have less than 37 hours per week of free time as compared to the more than 65 hours of free time for non-employed men, and employed women have less than 35 hours per week of free time as compared to the more than 51 hours per week among non-employed women.

Age

Variations by age are shown in Table 4.12 for both men and women separately. In general, time spent at work activities tends to be highest in the 30 to 59 age group, and drops off dramatically for those aged 60 and above. At the same time housework activities rise, especially for men and especially for household cleaning activities.

Men aged 60 and over also report more sleeping time. However, the highest sleep times are reported by young adults aged 18 to 24. In contrast, the 18–24 age group reports lowest time in personal care and eating activities; those in the 60–65 year age group spend the most time eating.

Child-care activity, not surprisingly, is highest for those in peak child-bearing and family years, namely among 25–29 and 30–39 year age groups. Time spent shopping is highest among 40–59 year age groups. Non-work transit is highest among 18–24 year olds and declines, although not monot-onically nor systematically, among older age groups.

In general, free time is lowest among middle-aged people. Education, not surprisingly, is highest among 18–29 year olds. Organizational activity, on the other hand, rises rather steadily with age.

Radio listening is highest among men aged 50 and older. Television time tends to parallel free time, with highest viewing times reported by those under 30 and over 50 (among men over age 60). Reading also tends to increase with increasing age, although not systematically.

Social life also tends to be higher among those under 30 and over 60. On the other hand, conversation time is much more constant with age. More time is spent by younger and older groups in regard to outdoor recreation and sports, but not invariably so. Hobby and other leisure activities are higher among older men, but not among older women.

The major Table 4.12 patterns by age, then, are found at the extremes. Adults under age 30 and over 60 tend to work less, sleep more, and have more free time (and use more of that free time to watch TV) than middle-aged groups. In addition, younger adults also travel more, do less housework, take more education courses, participate less in organizational activity, read less and spend more time socializing than those in older age groups.

Education

Time-use differences by education are shown in Table 4.13. It can be seen first that college educated men and women spend more time working than those with less formal education. This does not follow for housework; here college educated women spend less time doing almost all types of housework than high school educated women. College educated men spend as much time doing housework as high school educated men.

College educated men spend less than average time sleeping; college women spend more than average time sleeping. College educated women (and men) also spend less time resting. No systematic relations can be found between education and eating and personal care.

Nor are many notable or systematic relations found across the board between education and time spent on child care, shopping or non-work travel. College educated men do spend somewhat more time in non-work travel, and college educated women somewhat less time in child care. As a result mainly of longer work times, then, college educated men and women have less free time available than high school educated people (almost an hour less per day). College educated men and women spend much less time, therefore, in such free-time activities as television viewing and adult education. However, they spend as much or more time than high school educated people in organizational activity, reading, social life, conversation, outdoor recreation, hobbies and entertainment.

A major factor differentiating the lifestyles of college-educated people then, is the greater diversity of activities both in terms of work and of free-time activities. These activities mean they spend more time away from the home.

Marital Status

The differences by marital status in Table 4.14 are generally not as large as those found by employment status, age, or education. Thus, for example, married and non-married women differ hardly at all in terms of time spent at work. Married men spend about an hour per day more in work-related activities than do non-married men. However married men spend 20 minutes less time doing housework than do non-married men, while married women spend slightly more time doing housework than do non-married women.

Married women spend somewhat less time in personal care and eating than do non-married women, but they spend slightly more time sleeping

Table 4.13
1985 Jackson Time Use Differences by Sex and Education
(in hours per week; weighted by day of the week, age and sex)

Years in school	Men					Women					Total Sample
n=	0-11 (48)	12 (89)	13-15 (101)	16+ (63)	Total (301)	0-11 (43)	12 (130)	13-15 (115)	16+ (41)	Total (329)	(630)
1) Regular work	31.8	34.2	35.9	39.9	35.6	12.1	16.4	26.0	28.9	20.8	27.9
2) Second job	0.0	0.0	0.8	0.2	0.3	0.2	0.0	0.0	0.0	0.0	0.1
3) Non work	1.4	2.1	2.3	3.0	2.2	0.3	1.2	1.7	2.6	1.5	1.9
4) Trip to work	2.4	3.1	3.0	3.0	3.0	1.0	1.4	2.2	2.2	1.7	2.3
Work Related	35.7	39.4	42.0	46.4	41.2	13.8	19.0	30.0	33.7	24.0	32.2
5) Preparing food	1.0	1.6	2.3	1.6	1.7	6.1	6.5	5.7	5.1	5.9	4.0
6) Cleaning house	2.9	3.3	3.1	2.3	3.0	6.8	7.9	6.4	4.8	6.9	5.0
7) Laundry	0.7	0.3	0.6	0.3	0.5	2.7	2.0	2.0	1.5	2.0	1.3
8) Other housekeeping	3.1	2.9	2.8	3.3	3.0	1.7	1.9	1.9	1.4	1.7	2.3
9) Gardening, pets	0.5	0.2	0.2	0.1	0.2	0.3	0.7	0.5	0.3	0.5	0.5
Housework	8.3	8.3	9.3	7.7	8.5	17.6	18.9	16.4	13.1	17.1	13.1
10) Child care	0.7	0.7	0.9	0.9	0.8	3.6	3.1	2.9	2.8	3.1	2.0
11) Shopping	1.3	2.4	2.6	2.6	2.3	3.8	4.8	4.5	3.7	4.4	3.4
12) Non-work trips	5.7	5.2	7.9	6.2	6.4	6.3	7.8	7.5	7.0	7.3	6.9
Family Tasks	7.7	8.4	11.4	9.7	9.6	13.9	15.7	14.9	13.6	14.9	12.4

13) Sleep	55.4	55.1	52.6	49.9	53.2	54.4	53.5	51.7	55.6	53.2	53.2
14) Personal care	6.1	6.8	7.8	7.5	7.1	9.6	8.9	10.1	8.7	9.3	8.3
15) Eating	6.3	6.6	6.8	8.4	7.0	9.3	7.1	6.8	7.2	7.3	7.1
Personal Needs	67.8	68.5	67.2	65.8	67.3	73.3	69.5	68.6	71.5	69.8	68.6
16) Education	4.1	1.4	1.9	0.8	1.9	5.1	1.4	3.7	0.6	2.6	2.2
17) Organizations	0.7	2.3	1.7	1.6	1.7	1.5	1.6	2.1	5.0	2.1	2.0
18) Radio	1.0	1.0	0.1	0.2	0.6	0.2	0.1	0.2	0.0	0.1	0.3
19) Television	23.6	21.3	15.4	15.3	18.2	21.7	19.9	13.3	9.4	16.4	17.4
20) Reading	2.3	2.4	3.5	4.0	3.0	2.9	2.4	3.4	5.5	3.3	3.1
21) Social life	9.3	5.4	8.2	6.6	7.2	7.6	10.1	6.1	7.2	8.0	7.6
22) Conversation	2.3	1.3	1.5	3.0	1.9	3.1	2.7	3.3	2.7	2.9	2.4
23) Walking	0.5	1.0	0.9	0.3	0.8	0.5	0.1	0.1	0.2	0.1	0.5
24) Sports	0.6	3.4	1.6	2.2	2.1	0.9	1.3	1.7	1.4	1.4	1.7
25) Various leisure	0.7	1.0	0.9	2.0	1.2	2.0	1.2	1.6	2.1	2.0	1.6
26) Spectacles	0.0	0.2	0.7	0.3	0.3	1.3	0.7	0.5	0.2	0.7	0.5
27) Resting	3.5	2.4	1.4	2.0	2.2	2.2	2.4	2.0	1.3	2.1	2.1
Total Free Time #1	48.6	43.3	37.9	38.4	41.2	49.5	41.3	38.0	35.9	42.0	41.6
Free Time #2	49.6	42.5	38.7	37.8	41.4	47.4	43.7	37.3	35.9	40.9	41.2
Total Time	168	168	168	168	168	168	168	168	168	168	168

Table 4.14
1985 Jackson Time Use Differences by Sex and Marital Status
(in hours per week; weighted by day of the week, age and sex)

n=	Men Married (181)	Non-Married (120)	Total (301)	Women Married (178)	Non-Married (151)	Total (329)	TOTAL SAMPLE (630)
1) Regular work	38.1	31.7	35.6	21.2	20.3	20.8	27.9
2) Second job	0.5	0.1	0.3	0.0	0.1	0.0	0.1
3) Non work	2.6	1.9	2.2	1.4	1.5	1.4	1.9
4) Trip to work	3.4	2.7	3.0	1.6	1.7	1.7	2.3
Work Related	44.4	36.3	41.2	24.8	23.7	24.0	32.2
5) Preparing food	1.5	2.1	1.7	6.5	5.4	5.9	4.0
6) Cleaning house	2.6	3.6	3.0	6.9	6.9	4.5	5.0
7) Laundry	0.2	0.9	0.5	2.2	1.7	2.0	1.3
8) Other house-keeping	3.0	2.9	3.0	1.9	1.6	1.7	2.3
9) Gardening, pets	0.2	0.3	0.2	0.5	0.6	0.6	0.5
Housework	7.6	9.9	8.5	17.8	16.3	17.1	13.1
10) Child care	1.3	0.2	0.8	3.1	3.0	3.1	2.0
11) Shopping	2.6	2.0	2.3	4.9	3.8	4.4	3.4
12) Non-work trips	5.9	7.2	6.4	6.6	8.3	7.3	7.0
Family Tasks	9.7	9.4	9.6	14.7	15.3	14.9	12.4
13) Sleep	52.8	53.7	53.2	54.1	52.3	53.2	53.2
14) Personal care	7.0	7.3	7.1	8.5	10.4	9.3	8.3
15) Eating	7.3	6.4	7.0	6.8	7.8	7.3	7.1
Personal Needs	67.1	67.4	67.3	69.4	70.5	69.8	68.6
16) Education	0.6	3.8	1.9	1.2	4.3	2.6	2.2
17) Organizations	2.6	0.5	1.7	2.6	1.7	2.2	2.0
18) Radio	0.7	0.7	0.7	0.2	0.1	0.1	0.3
19) Television	17.8	19.0	18.3	17.3	15.5	16.4	17.4
20) Reading	3.3	2.9	3.0	3.6	2.7	3.3	3.1
21) Social life	5.5	9.8	7.2	7.7	8.4	8.0	7.6
22) Conversation	2.0	1.7	1.9	2.9	2.9	2.9	2.4
23) Walking	0.6	1.0	0.8	0.1	0.2	0.1	0.5
24) Sports	2.6	1.3	2.1	1.4	1.3	1.4	1.7
25) Various leisure	1.2	1.2	1.2	1.9	2.1	2.0	1.6
26) Spectacles	0.2	0.5	0.3	0.5	0.8	0.7	0.5
27) Resting	2.1	2.3	2.2	2.3	2.0	2.1	2.1
Total Free Time #1	39.0	44.8	41.3	41.8	42.2	42.0	41.6
Free Time #2	38.8	45.0	41.4	39.7	42.5	40.9	41.2
Total Time	168	168	168	168	168	168	168

and resting. Married men spend slightly less time sleeping and slightly more time eating than do non-married men.

Married men spend more time in child-care activities and shopping, but less time in non-work travel. Married women also spend more time shopping and less time in travel than non-married women; but, surprisingly, they also spend no more time in child-care activities.

While married men have close to an hour less free time per day than non-married men, the free time of married and non-married women is about equal. Non-married men spend more of their additional free time on adult education, social life, entertainment and walking; married men spend more time on organizational activities and sports. Non-married women also spend more of their free time in walking, entertainment, educational and social activities; married women spend slightly more time in organizational activities and watching television.

The activity patterns of married and non-married women are surprisingly similar. Mainly as a result of their shorter work hours, non-married men can spend more time in certain out-of-home activities, particularly in adult education and socializing.

Summary, Comparisons and Conclusions

Comparison of the daily time budgets of residents in Pskov and in Jackson has shown many similarities in the daily activity patterns of the U.S. and USSR; however, some of the most important differences in activities occur mainly because of the specific background conditions of work in the two countries. The most direct comparison of data in Pskov and Jackson is thus obtained when we compare the working populations in Tables 4.4 and 4.11, and in summary form in Table 4.15.

As one can see, the time differences between employed men in both Pskov and in Jackson are not strong. While the working time (with overtime and second jobs included) in Pskov is only 1.4 hours per week longer than in Jackson, differences in work-related activities amount to four hours per week, mainly due to the longer commuting times needed to work in Pskov.

Our study has found that the general amounts of time spent by men on housework and meeting personal needs in Pskov and Jackson is practically the same. Employed Soviet men do more household work related to meal preparation and child care, while American men spend more time grooming and shopping. Non-work transit in Jackson totals almost two hours higher than in Pskov.

The total amount of time spent on physiological needs, outside of resting, differs only by 2 percent, although employed men in Pskov spend

Table 4.15
General Differences in Time Use in Pskov and Jackson
(in hours per week)

Types of activity	Employed Men			Employed Women		
	Pskov	Jackson	Difference	Pskov	Jackson	Difference
n=	(797)	(237)		(1056)	(202)	
Work	43.5	42.1	−1.4	40.0	35.3	−4.7
Work-related	10.0	6.1	−3.9	8.0	5.3	−2.7
Housework	10.5	10.7	+0.2	22.0	17.5	−4.5
Personal Care	64.8	66.3	+1.5	66.4	67.8	+1.4
Free time	34.5	36.7	+2.2	26.5	34.6	+8.1
Non-work trips	4.6	6.1	±1.5	5.0	7.3	±2.3
Total:	168	168	0	168	168	0

more time sleeping than men in Jackson, and less time on personal hygiene and grooming and eating.

Amount of free time available to employed men in both cities is also very much the same (34.5 hours per week in Pskov and 36.7 hours in Jackson). Employed men in Jackson spend more time in organizational activities (especially attending religious services) and TV viewing. Men in Pskov do more reading, walking outdoors, and visiting cultural and recreation events, especially the movies.

On the other hand, the study has found that the daily schedules of employed women in Pskov and Jackson differ more than those of men. First of all, employed women in Jackson have an almost five hour shorter workweek than Pskov women due mainly to the fact that in the USSR all working residents are fully employed, while in the U.S. substantial proportions of employed men and women work less than 35 hours per week. Employed women in Jackson also spend more than two hours less time in the commute to work.

Employed women in Jackson spend four hours less time on household activities than do the women of Pskov. In contrast, they spend more time on physiological needs and have eight hours more free time; time spent in non-work travel is also two hours longer in Jackson. Again, these differences in the increased housework time spent each week for daily needs and for free time may be explained by the fact that the workweeks of employed women in the U.S. are shorter than in the USSR. American non-employed women do more housework but also have additional free time.

Considering specific housework-related activities, we find that employed women in Pskov spend about eight hours per week preparing food and meals, while those in Jackson spend only four hours; non-employed women in the two cities spend 10.5 and 8.4 hours per week in housework, respectively. Employed women in Pskov spend four hours per week mending clothes and laundry compared to less than two hours in Jackson. Employed women in Pskov do more child care (three hours) than employed women in Jackson (two hours). Employed American women do the same amount of house cleaning (4–5 hours per week) as those in Pskov. Employed women in Jackson spend four hours per week in shopping and using various services, while employed Soviet women spend three hours on such activities.

Employed women in Pskov spend more time sleeping (55 hours per week) than those in Jackson (53 hours per week), but employed American women spend slightly more time for personal care and eating than Soviet women.

There are certain differences in the structure of free time as well. For example, employed women in Jackson spend more time in organizational activities (mainly religious services), TV viewing, social interaction, conversation and sports. On the other hand, employed Soviet women spend more time reading, walking outdoors, and relaxing.

Demographic factors have almost the same effect on time-use patterns in Pskov and in Jackson. Differences between the young and middle-aged, educated and less educated, or married and non-married residents are consistent enough that one can almost predict the differences in one city by simply knowing the differences in the other.

It is interesting that most of the differences in types of activities found in the two cities in the 1960s (Patrushev 1974) are found again in the 1980s. However, in the next chapter, we will also find that there are some differences is the two sites that were hardly discernible twenty years ago.

5

Historical Trends:
1965–1986

The data in Chapter 3 identified many similarities and some differences between Jackson and Pskov in regard to background factors. Chapter 4 reviewed how some of these factors affected daily use of time. In this chapter, we review these factors in a more directly comparative context, in particular as they appear to have changed across time in both societies. The first set of comparisons involve personal background factors, the second the time-use differences. The changes in Pskov are reviewed first.

Changes in Pskov

Background Factors

The sex ratio in Pskov remained approximately the same as in 1965; the age structure, however, changed more significantly. The percentage of young people aged 18–24 grew from 13 percent to 17 percent, and also those aged 50–65 years from 17 percent to 24 percent; on the other hand, the percentage of middle-aged groups of the population decreased somewhat. The exact figures can be seen in the first two columns of Table 5.1.

The percentage of married people also decreased somewhat, from 76 percent to 72 percent, while the percentage of those divorced grew from 3 percent to 9 percent. More than half of those surveyed considered themselves the head of the family; in 1965 it was 53 percent, in 1986 it was 51 percent. About one-third were spouses of the head of household (in 1965, 34 percent; in 1986, 27 percent).

About eight out of ten of those surveyed in both years lived in households of two to four persons; similarly, there was no significant change in the number of persons working in the family. The number having children under 18 years of age decreased. In 1965, 32 percent had no children, and in 1986, 43 percent; while 42 percent had one child in 1965, in 1986, that figure was 35 percent; the figures for 2–3 children were 25 percent and 22 percent, respectively. Thus, the presence of children in the family declined somewhat over the last twenty years.

The educational level of the population over these twenty years rose

Table 5.1
Cross-Time Differences in Background Factors: Pskov

	Pskov			Pskov	
	1965	1986		1965	1986
Sex:			**Children:**		
Male	42	44	None	32	43
Female	58	56	One	42	35
	100	100	Two-Three	25	20
Employment:			Four+	1	2
Yes	91	85		100	100
No	9	15	**Married:**		
	100	100	Yes	76	72
Age:			No	24	28
18–24	13	17		100	100
25–29	19	16	**Sex-Marital Status:**		
30–39	30	25	Unmarried Men	5	6
40–49	21	18	Married Men	36	34
50–59	14	17	Unmarried Women	19	20
60–65	3	7	Married Women	41	40
66+	0	X		100	100
	100	100	**Sex-Employment Status:**		
Education:			Unemployed Men	0	4
0–6 Yrs	26	7	Employed Men	42	39
7–9 Yrs	28	16	Unemployed Women	8	12
10–11 Yrs	17	30	Employed Women	50	45
Technical	16	27		100	100
College	11	20			
	100	100	**Distance to City Center**		
			<1 Km	31	32
HHsize:			1–2 Km	43	29
One	5	8	2–5 Km	17	32
Two	15	21	5–10 Km	7	5
Three	33	26	10–20 Km	3	2
Four	30	26	20+ Km	0	0
Five	12	8		100	100
Six+	5	5			
	100	100	**Amenities:**		
			Running water	64	90
Employed in HH:			Garden	25	37
None	0	2	Automobile	2	20
One	17	22	Scooter	11	14
Two	64	55	Bicycle	29	30
Three+	20	21	Radio	94	92
	100	100	TV	49	98
			Books (100+)	14	41
			Telephone	11	23

significantly. Thus, the percentage of those surveyed having less than seven grades of schooling in 1965 in Pskov was 26 percent and in 1986, 7 percent; incomplete secondary education was 28 percent in 1965 and 16 percent in 1986. Those with secondary education (including special training schools) grew from 33 percent in 1965 to 57 percent in 1986. The number with some college education rose from 11 percent to 20 percent.

The overwhelming proportion among those surveyed both in 1965 (91 percent) and in 1986 (85 percent) were employed in the paid labor force. However, the proportion of non-working people grew somewhat because of increases in the numbers of retired persons (from 2 percent to 6 percent), the disabled, students and those temporarily between jobs. Although not shown in Table 5.1, the percentage of full-time housewives decreased from 4 percent to less than 1 percent. In examining those surveyed by branches of the economy, 36 percent of all those working in 1965 were working in manufacturing industry and 40 percent in 1986. In trade and consumer services, the proportions were 8 percent and 16 percent, respectively, and in public services, transport and communications, the figures were 18 percent earlier and 9 percent in 1986.

In early 1965, there was a six-day workweek, with one day off. Later in 1965, a change to a five-day workweek was implemented, with the exception of employees working in schools, post-secondary educational institutions and a small number of enterprises and institutions (where the six-day work week was preserved). In 1986, 9 percent had a six-day workweek and some 83 percent worked the five-day workweek; 80 percent of employees worked a single day shift.

The living conditions of these urban residents changed significantly. Whereas in 1965, 29 percent of those surveyed in Pskov lived in houses with one or two units, in 1986 the figure was 9 percent; the proportion living in apartment houses grew from 67 percent to 84 percent. The extensive growth of industry led to a growth in the number of those living in dormitories, from 3 percent to 7 percent.

Among those surveyed, the percentage of those living in industrial and non-industrial outskirts of the city grew because of expansion of the boundaries of the city and new construction. As a result, the distance from home to the center of the city grew somewhat.

The growth of urban construction led to a decrease in the number of inhabitants who had their own plots of land around their houses. Whereas in 1965 about 21 percent of those surveyed had plots, in 1986 this percentage was a mere 8 percent. However, 26 percent had a piece of land in a garden cooperative, or had a summer house with a plot of land. Overall, then, the total number of those having a plot of land grew from approximately 25 percent to 37 percent over the course of twenty years.

The situation with municipal conveniences (electricity, water, etc.) has also improved. About 90 percent of those surveyed in 1986 had all municipal conveniences, while in 1965 only 40 percent did.

While the proportion of respondents owning bicycles, motorcycles (scooters, mopeds) grew only three percentage points over twenty years, the number of those having personal automobiles grew in Pskov by a factor of ten—from 2 percent to 20 percent.

Access to mass communication also increased significantly. The proportions owning more than 100 books in 1965 was 14 percent; by 1986, that figure had risen to 41 percent. In 1965 only about half of those surveyed had television sets; in 1986, practically all Pskov residents did, with 73 percent having black and white sets and 42 percent color sets.

Time-Use Differences in Pskov

Many of the changes which have taken place in the living conditions, cultural growth and everyday needs of the Soviet people are reflected in the use of time. As summarized in Table 5.2, however, these changes, insofar as the amount of time consumed by work-related activity is concerned, are insignificant. This is because the norm for working time has not changed in the USSR for the past twenty years. Supplementary paid work (a second job) is relatively rare in 1986, as it was in 1965. Despite the significant improvements in transport facilities, the workers of Pskov (as in other cities in the country) still report longer travel times to and from the workplace.

Household work and the satisfaction of familial needs continue to require significant expenditures of time. However, on average for each resident of Pskov, they have been reduced by almost three hours a week. Among working men, they have increased somewhat; but among working women, housework has been rather significantly reduced by almost seven hours per week per capita. Expenditures of time for family and household obligations by people who are not employed have also been reduced. This reduction is reflected in the expenditures of time for all forms of activity connected with housework and the satisfaction of household needs, as will be seen in the more detailed calculations in Table 5.3. Thus, among working women expenditures of time on food preparation have been reduced by about one and a half hours per week per capita, on house cleaning by about two hours, on the care of clothing and linens by just over an hour, and on shopping and consumer services by about half an hour.

As a result of these changes in expenditures of time, then, there have been two contrasting trends: a reduction in the total workload of working women of seven hours a week as compared to an increase of one hour a week among working men. The time freed by this reduction of the work-

Table 5.2
Time Use Differences in Pskov: 1965-1986
(in hours per week; weighted by day of the week, age and sex)

	Employed Men		Employed Women		Non- Employed Women	
	1965	1986	1965	1986	1965	1986
n=	(1097)	(797)	(1574)	(1056)	(201)	(250)
WORK	43.4	43.5	39.9	40.0	1.4	0.5
Work-related	4.9	4.8	4.2	3.8	0	0.4
Work commute	4.9	5.2	4.2	4.2	0	0.1
HOUSEWORK*	9.8	10.5	28.7	22.0	41.2	36.9
PERSONAL NEEDS	65.4	64.9	64.4	66.4	72.8	72.1
FREE TIME	34.3	34.5	21.0	26.5	44.1	51.0
Non-work trips	5.6	4.6	5.6	5.0	8.4	7.0
TOTAL HOURS	168	168	168	168	168	168
*Housework Subtotals						
Preparing food	1.4	2.5	9.1	7.6	12.6	10.5
Cleaning house	4.2	4.0	7.0	4.7	11.8	8.5
Laundry	0	0.3	4.9	3.6	5.6	5.0
Gardening	1.4	0.3	0.7	0.1	2.8	0.3
Child care	1.4	1.6	3.5	3.2	4.2	9.2
Shopping	1.4	1.8	3.5	2.9	4.2	3.4
	9.8	10.5	28.7	22.0	41.2	36.9

load has gone in some part to the satisfaction of personal needs, but mainly to increased free time. This resulting increase in women's free time can be regarded as a major social transformation.

The changes in time expenditures on the satisfaction of physiological needs (sleeping, eating, grooming) is relatively small. For working men it is essentially unchanged, while for working women it has grown by two hours a week, or by about 3 percent.

Over the last twenty years, free time has increased overall by three hours per week, with working women having a 6.7 hour increase. For employed men, on the other hand, it remains practically unchanged. As a result, the difference in the amount of free time at the disposal of working men and women has been reduced from 63 percent to only 30 percent in 1986.

Table 5.3
Time Use Differences in Pskov: 1965-1986
(in hours per week)

	Men		Women			
	Employed		Employed		Non Employed	
	1965	1986	1965	1986	1965	1986
	(1097)	(797)	(1574)	(1056)	(201)	(250)
1) Regular work	43.4	43.4	39.9	39.9	.7	.4
2) Second job	0	.1	0	.2	0	.1
3) Non work	4.9	4.8	4.2	3.8	0	.4
4) Trip to work	4.9	5.2	4.2	4.2	0	.1
Work Related	53.2	53.5	48.3	48.2	.7	1.0
5) Preparing food	1.4	2.5	9.1	7.6	12.6	10.5
6) Cleaning house	1.4	1.4	5.6	3.9	9.8	6.9
7) Laundry	0	.3	4.9	3.6	5.6	5.0
8) Other housekeeping	2.8	2.6	1.4	.8	1.4	1.6
9) Gardening, pets	1.4	.3	.7	.1	2.8	.3
Housework	7.0	7.2	21.7	16.0	32.0	24.3
10) Childcare	1.4	1.6	3.5	3.2	4.2	9.2
11)Shopping	1.4	1.8	3.5	2.9	4.2	3.4
12) Non work trips	5.6	4.6	5.6	5.0	8.4	7.0
Family Tasks	8.4	7.9	12.6	11.1	16.8	18.6
13) Sleep	53.9	53.5	53.2	54.6	58.8	58.0
14) Personal care	5.6	6.0	5.6	6.6	6.3	6.4
15) Eating	5.6	5.3	5.6	5.2	7.7	7.6
Personal Needs	65.1	64.9	64.4	66.3	72.8	72.1
16) Resting	2.1	3.4	1.4	2.4	4.2	5.4
17) Education	4.9	.7	3.5	.8	12.6	8.2
18) Organizations	.7	1.2	.7	.7	.7	.6
19) Radio	1.4	.2	.7	.1	1.4	.1
20) Television	5.6	14.5	3.5	10.7	7.0	13.6
21) Reading	7.7	5.8	4.2	3.5	7.0	6.1
22) Social life	2.8	2.6	1.4	2.1	2.1	4.0
23) Conversation	1.4	1.2	.7	1.3	2.1	2.3
24) Walking	3.5	1.5	1.4	1.4	2.1	4.2
25) Sports	1.4	1.8	0	.6	.7	.3
26) Various leisure	.7	.8	1.4	2.3	2.1	5.7
27) Spectacles	2.1	.9	2.1	.6	2.8	.6
+ Free Time	34.3	34.5	21.0	26.5	44.8	51.0

* Less time .05 hours per week
+ Excludes travel related to free time

The structure of free time has also changed considerably. Time spent viewing television has increased almost by a factor of three. Whereas in 1965 TV took up about 16 percent of free time, the figure in 1986 is about 40 percent; for working men television consumes over 14 hours per week, and for women about 11 hours. This increased expenditure of time on television viewing has taken place *not* by an increase in the average actual length of viewing per viewer, but by a significant expansion of the television audience: whereas in 1965 less than 40 percent of working people viewed some television broadcast on the diary day, in 1986 the figure was well over 80 percent.

Another significant change is the reduction of time spent in adult education. This may be a result of the rise in the educational level of the population which reduces the need for taking such courses. At the same time, reductions are also found in the time spent on visits to movie theaters and other institutions of culture, on reading of printed matter, and on listening to the radio (as a primary activity). On the other hand, in 1986 free-time activities involving physical exertion (recreation, sports, walking) take up less than 10 percent of free time for the working population, much as they did in 1965.

This is the general picture of the changes which have taken place in the use of time by the inhabitants of the city of Pskov over the course of twenty years. These changes on the whole should be regarded as positive: the total workload of working women has been reduced, and their free time has increased. Working men have begun to take a somewhat larger part in the housework and family care. Nonetheless, expenditures of time on family household obligations by women is still rather large. And the free time devoted to television means that more passive forms of time expenditure now predominate.

Changes in Jackson

Background Factors

The sex ratio in Jackson remained approximately the same as in 1965, although there were more women in 1965. The age structure, however, changed more significantly. On the one hand, compared to 1965 the percentage of young people aged 18–24 grew from 14 percent to 22, and also those aged 60–65 years (from 7 percent to 12 percent); on the other hand, the percentage of middle-aged groups of the population has decreased somewhat. The exact figures can be seen in the first two columns of Table 5.4.

The percentage of married people decreased markedly, from 86 percent to 58 percent, with the percentage of divorced (not shown) growing from 4

Table 5.4
Cross-Time Differences in Background Factors: Jackson (in Percentages)

	Jackson			Jackson	
	1965	1986		1965	1986
Sex:			Children:		
Male	49	46	None	34	48
Female	51	54	One	18	13
	100	100	Two-Three	34	28
			Four+	13	11
Employment:				100	100
Yes	71	70			
No	29	30	Married:		
	100	100	Yes	86	58
			No	14	42
Age:				100	100
18–24	14	22			
25–29	14	14	Sex-Marital Status:		
30–39	19	19	Non-Married Men	6	19
40–49	28	17	Married Men	42	29
50–59	18	16	Non-Married Women	8	24
60–65	7	12	Married Women	44	28
	100	100		100	100
			Sex-Employment Status:		
Education:			Unemployed Men	1	8
Primary	13	2	Employed Men	47	40
Some sec.	28	13	Unemployed Women	28	22
Secondary	48	35	Employed Women	24	30
Some college	12	35		100	100
College grad	8	15	Distance to City Center		
	100	100	<1 Km	8	15
HHsize:			1–2 Km	19	29
One	4	6	2–5 Km	21	30
Two	20	31	5–10 Km	16	25
Three	22	21	10–20 Km	2	2
Four	22	20	20+ Km	16	0
Five	17	8		100	100
Six+	15	4			
	100	100	Amenities:		
			Running water	99	98
Employed in HH:			Garden	21	48
None	0	16	Automobile	92	94
One	55	38	Scooter	X	22
Two	35	36	Bicycle	X	64
Three+	10	10	Radio	98	98
	100	100	TV	97	98
			Books (100+)	23	38
			Telephone	90	96
			House	90	71
			Apartment	5	22

percent to 12 percent. More than half of those surveyed considered themselves the head of the family. In 1965, it was 53 percent, in 1986, it was 55 percent. Less than a third were spouses of the head (in 1965, 34 percent; in 1986, 29 percent).

Approximately 72 percent of those surveyed in 1986 lived in households of two to four people, while 64 percent did so in 1965. There was a significant difference in the number of persons working in the family—but that was mainly because unemployed single individuals were not included in the 1965 sample frame. However, the number having children under 18 years of age decreased. In 1965, 34 percent had no children, and in 1986, 48 percent; while 18 percent had one child in 1965, in 1986, that figure was 13 percent; the figures for 2–3 children were 34 percent and 28 percent, respectively. Thus, the presence of children in the family declined somewhat over the last twenty years.

The education level of the population over these twenty years rose significantly. Thus, the percentage of those surveyed having less than twelve grades of schooling in 1965 in Jackson was 41 percent (in 1986, 15 percent); those who had completed secondary education only was 48 percent in 1965 and 35 percent in 1986. Those with at least some college education (including community colleges) grew from 20 percent in 1965 to 50 percent in 1986. The number of college graduates rose from 8 percent to 15 percent.

Just over two-thirds of those surveyed both in 1965 and in 1986 were employed in the paid labor force. However, the proportion of non-working people grew somewhat, mainly because of the increases allowed in the sample of retired persons, the disabled, and students. The percentage of full-time housewives decreased from more than 40 percent to 15 percent. In examining those surveyed by branches of the economy, 35 percent of all those working in 1965 were working in manufacturing industry; the figure was 36 percent in 1986. In trade and consumer services, the proportions were 8 percent and 16 percent, respectively and in public services, transport and communications, the figures were 18 percent earlier and 9 percent in 1986.

The living conditions of these urban residents also changed significantly. Whereas in 1965, 90 percent of those surveyed in Jackson lived in houses with one or two families, in 1986 the figure was 71 percent; the proportion living in apartment houses grew from 5 percent to 22 percent. As a result of the urbanized sampling frame employed in 1986, the typical distance from home to the center of the city was much shorter. Whereas 18 percent of 1965 respondents lived more than 10 kilometers from the center of Jackson in 1965, less than 2 percent did in 1986.

The growth of urban construction led to an increase in the number of inhabitants who had their own plots of land around their houses. Whereas in 1965 about 21 percent of those surveyed had plots, in 1986 this percentage was 48 percent. The situation with municipal conveniences (electricity, water, etc.) has remained well over 90 percent, as did the proportion owning automobiles, TV sets and radios. The number of those having access to more than 100 books in their home in 1965 was 23 percent; by 1986, that figure had risen to 38 percent.

Time Use Changes in Jackson

Table 5.5 examines the cross-time differences in activity patterns in the 1966 and 1986 Jackson data, with results given in hours per week. Non-employed men are excluded from the analysis as they were in 1966. It is important to remember that only people in the Jackson urbanized area are in the 1986 data, and not those who live further away.

Table 5.5
Time Use Differences in Jackson: 1966-1986
(in hours per week; weighted by day of the week, age and sex)

	Employed Men		Employed Women		Non Employed Women	
n=	1966 (354)	1986 (252)	1966 (187)	1986 (188)	1966 (227)	1986 (141)
WORK	42.8	42.1	34.8	35.4	1.1	1.5
Work-related	4.0	2.6	3.1	2.5	0	0
Work commute	3.7	3.5	2.3	2.9	.1	.1
HOUSEWORK*	8.5	10.8	24.4	17.4	47.1	34.6
PERSONAL NEEDS	68.3	66.2	70.1	67.9	72.1	72.8
FREE TIME	34.6	36.8	26.9	34.6	40.3	51.7
Non-work trips	6.1	6.1	6.4	7.3	7.4	7.5
TOTAL HOURS	168	168	168	168	168	168
*Housework Subtotals						
Preparing food	.9	1.7	5.3	4.1	11.4	8.6
Cleaning house	4.0	5.1	9.0	5.3	15.9	13.1
Laundry	.1	.6	3.3	1.5	6.7	3.6
Gardening	.3	.3	.3	.3	.5	.8
Child care	.8	.8	1.9	2.0	7.6	4.6
Shopping	2.4	2.3	4.6	4.2	5.1	4.8
	8.5	10.8	24.4	17.4	47.1	34.6

It can be seen first that times in regular work activities are very similar to those twenty years previous. Less time is reported in non-work activities at the workplace. The commute to work is slightly lower for employed men, and somewhat higher for employed women (from 2.3 to 2.9 hours per week) even though this sample lives closer to the center of downtown Jackson.

Housework times have increased for men across all activities except gardening and pet care. In contrast, women's housework times are generally lower, particularly for the "traditional" womens' responsibilities: cooking, cleaning and laundry.

Sleep time is one to five hours lower in 1986 than was found in 1966. Eating and meal time is also lower (except for non-employed women) and the same decline is found for resting time. Personal-care time, on the other hand, is up over an hour per week, especially for non-employed women.

Child care is about the same among employed men and women as it was in 1966; it is down considerably for non-labor force women. Shopping times are about the same as in 1966. Non-work trips are also about the same as in 1966 for employed men and non-employed women, and are up about an hour among employed women.

As a result of all these shifts, men have two more hours of free time. But employed women have almost eight more hours of free time, and non-labor-force women more than 11 additional hours of free time. The major free-time activity that has shown increased time is television viewing, up nearly three hours per week for men and more than seven hours per week for women. These details are shown in Table 5.6.

More free time is now spent in adult education, in walking, and in sports activities. The increase in sports activities among women is especially notable. Less free time is spent in social life and hobbies, but somewhat more time overall is spent in conversation.

National-level Changes

Table 5.7 presents some parallel analyses for national-level, time-diary data, conducted both in 1965 and in 1985. It should be noted that these are preliminary data for the first quarter's collection of 1985—and only for the spring and winter months. The activity coding schemes used are somewhat different as well. The data are thus not as comparable as in Table 5.6.

Nonetheless, we again find slight declines in men's work time, in second jobs and in non-work activities; women's work time is also down. As in Table 5.3, commuting time to and from work is about the same.

As in Table 5.6, men's housework time is up significantly, and women's housework is down significantly, especially for the core housework activities of cooking and cleaning. The rise in garden time is due in large part

Table 5.6
Comparison of 1986 and 1966 Time Use Results in Jackson
(in hours per week)

	Men Employed		Women Employed		Women Not Employed	
	1966	1986	1966	1986	1966	1986
n=	(313)	(252)	(178)	(188)	(186)	(141)
1) Regular work	42.8	41.8	35.3	35.3	1.1	1.5
2) Second job	0.4	0.3	.2	.1	0	0
3) Non work	4.0	2.6	3.1	2.4	*	*
4) Trip to work	3.7	3.5	2.3	2.9	.1	.1
Work Related	50.9	48.2	40.8	40.7	1.2	1.6
5) Preparing food	.9	1.7	5.3	4.1	11.4	8.5
6) Cleaning house	1.7	2.2	7.2	4.4	13.8	10.3
7) Laundry	.1	.6	3.3	1.5	6.7	2.6
8) Other housekeeping	2.3	2.7	1.8	1.0	2.1	2.8
9) Gardening, pets	.3	.2	.3	.3	.5	.8
Housework	5.3	7.6	17.9	11.3	34.5	25.0
10) Child care	.8	.8	1.9	2.0	7.5	4.6
11) Shopping	2.4	2.3	4.6	4.2	5.1	4.8
12) Non-work trips	6.1	6.1	6.4	7.3	7.4	7.5
Family Tasks	9.3	9.2	12.9	13.5	20.7	16.9
13) Sleep	53.5	52.6	55.0	52.7	58.8	53.9
14) Personal care	6.5	7.1	7.7	9.1	7.4	9.7
15) Eating	7.9	6.5	6.8	5.9	8.9	9.1
Personal Needs	67.9	66.2	69.5	67.7	72.1	72.8
16) Resting	2.4	2.1	2.3	1.6	4.0	2.6
17) Education	.7	.9	.5	1.6	.5	4.0
18) Organizations	1.7	1.7	1.9	2.3	2.7	2.0
19) Radio	.4	.6	.2	.3	.2	.2
20) Television	13.4	16.1	6.9	13.6	11.6	20.3
21) Reading	3.5	2.9	2.4	3.1	3.5	3.3
22) Social life	8.2	6.4	8.0	6.2	10.1	10.5
23) Conversation	1.2	1.9	1.9	2.4	3.6	3.6
24) Walking	.1	.6	.1	.1	.1	.3
25) Sports	1.5	2.1	.1	1.4	.1	1.3
26) Various leisure	1.2	1.0	1.7	1.3	3.1	2.9
27) Spectacles	.3	.3	.9	.6	.7	.7
Free Time	34.6	36.8	26.9	34.6	40.2	51.7

*Less than .05 hours per week.
Subtotals may not add to total because of rounding.

Table 5.7
Comparison of 1986 and 1966 Time Use Results Nationally
(in hours per week)

	MEN		WOMEN			
	Employed		Employed		Not Employed	
	1965	1985	1965	1985	1965	1985
n=	(506)	(437)	(305)	(403)	(386)	(239)
1) Regular work	43.7	41.0	34.9	33.1	.8	2.5
2) Second job	1.1	.5	.4	.2	.1	.6
3) Non work	4.1	2.4	3.6	2.2	.1	.2
4) Trip to work	4.9	4.9	3.6	3.6	.2	.7
Work Related	53.8	48.8	42.5	39.1	1.2	4.0
5) Preparing food	.9	1.4	5.5	4.9	10.6	7.3
6) Cleaning house	1.2	2.3	7.3	4.9	13.6	9.8
7) Laundry	.2	.2	3.1	1.8	6.7	2.1
8) Other housekeeping	1.9	2.4	1.5	1.6	2.8	1.9
9) Gardening, pets	.3	.8	.3	.7	.6	1.1
Housework	4.5	7.1	17.7	13.9	34.3	22.2
10) Childcare	.6	.6	2.1	2.0	7.4	3.9
11) Shopping	2.9	2.6	3.4	3.2	4.8	5.1
12) Non work trips	5.7	6.9	5.0	7.1	7.2	8.1
Family Tasks	9.2	10.1	10.5	12.3	19.4	17.1
13) Sleep	52.5	53.5	53.3	53.3	54.2	55.5
14) Personal	6.8	7.5	9.0	10.5	7.7	10.4
15) Eating	8.5	7.4	6.6	7.0	8.8	9.3
Personal Needs	67.8	68.4	68.9	70.8	71.7	75.2
16) Resting	1.8	2.2	2.6	2.5	2.6	4.5
17) Education	1.0	.6	.7	1.3	1.9	2.5
18) Organizations	1.4	.9	1.3	1.5	2.8	1.8
19) Radio	.5	.3	.5	.1	.3	.7
20) Television	11.5	14.6	7.3	11.7	10.9	18.2
21) Reading	4.1	2.6	2.7	2.4	3.9	3.7
22) Social life	7.1	5.3	7.5	5.1	10.4	6.4
23) Conversation	1.5	2.2	2.0	2.8	3.6	5.0
24) Walking	.2	.5	.1	.5	.2	1.1
25) Sports	1.3	2.0	.5	1.4	.4	1.6
26) Various leisure	1.2	1.6	2.0	1.6	3.6	2.7
27) Spectacles	1.2	1.0	1.2	.9	.8	1.2
Free Time	32.8	33.6	28.4	31.9	41.4	49.3

to the spring planting season during which many of the 1985 interviews were conducted.

Time spent sleeping and resting is up slightly from the 1965 national study, unlike the slight decline in Table 5.6. Personal-care time is up and eating time is down for men and up for women.

As with the Jackson data in Table 5.6, child care time is down significantly for non-employed women and about the same for employed women. Shopping time is about the same in 1985 as in 1965. Non-work trips are up one to two hours per week.

Again, the end result is that people had more free time in 1985 than in 1965, particularly so for non-employed women. The major recipient of that free time for employed men, employed women and homemakers was television. Adult education (mainly for women), conversations, walking, and sports also showed some increase in 1985. Organizational activity, reading, visiting and hobbies (for women) were all down from 1965 levels.

These preliminary national results tend to confirm many of the trends suggested in the Table 5.6 analysis of the Jackson 1966–1986 trends. The main change is in the decreased housework times of women. The result has been an increase in free time, especially for non-employed women. These 1966–1986 trends, then, are not just confined to our small sample in Jackson, but hold for U.S. national samples as well.

Summary, Comparisons and Conclusions

Personal Factors

There are several interesting ways in which figures for Pskov compare to Jackson. First, the ratio of women to men over the last 20 years has become more even in the two survey sites. The proportion of men declined slightly (from 49 percent to 46 percent) in Jackson, while it rose slightly (from 42 percent to 44 percent) in Pskov. Part of this is due to different social processes in the two cities, as the sex ratio has evened out in Pskov after the loss of many men during World War II and as more men leave Jackson for better job opportunities in other parts of the United States.

The ratio of employed women to non-employed women has also become more similar, as more American women work and more Russian women have time off for child-rearing purposes or because of early retirement (age 55 for women, age 60 for men). Nonetheless, it is still true that far more women in Pskov (80 percent) have paid jobs as compared to women in Jackson (58 percent).

The major age shifts across time occur for young adults. The proportion of 18–24 year olds has risen from 14 percent to 22 percent in Jackson and from 13 percent to 17 percent in Pskov. There are also relatively more older people as well; the 50–65 age group rose from 25 percent to 28 percent in Jackson, and from 17 percent to 24 percent in Pskov. While this means there are still relatively more middle-aged people in Pskov than Jackson, the age distribution across the two sites remains rather similar.

Far greater shifts can be found in the rising educational levels in the two countries. The proportion of Jackson respondents with at least some post-secondary school education has risen from 20 percent to 50 percent in Jackson, and from 27 percent to 47 percent in Pskov. Again, direct comparisons of educational level across the two sites must be done with extreme caution because of the substantial differences in educational structure between the two countries. Nonetheless, it is clear that these are major shifts in one of the most important determinants of time use.

The number of residents per dwelling has also declined in both sites, but for different reasons. The proportion of single occupancy households has risen from 4 percent to 16 percent in Jackson and from 5 percent to 8 percent in Pskov. The large increase in Jackson is due to the much higher proportion of unmarried men and women in 1986 (42 percent) than in 1965 (14 percent); in Pskov, these proportions have remained quite stable. The proportion of respondents living in households with five or more occupants, on the other hand, has declined from 32 percent to 12 percent in Jackson and from 17 percent to 13 percent in Pskov. The number of households without an employed person is sharply higher in Jackson in 1986, but that is largely because such households were excluded from the 1965 sampling frame.

The proportion of respondents without children has also risen notably since 1965, going from 34 percent to 48 percent in Jackson and from 32 percent to 43 percent in Pskov. However, the proportion of respondents with three or more children is still higher in Jackson.

Pskov residents continue to live closer to the center of the city than Jackson residents, even though more Pskov residents live further from the center in 1986 and the 1986 Jackson sample was restricted to the urbanized area and not the broad area covered in 1965 (which actually extended beyond the Jackson county boundaries). As is the case of the education variable, the marked differences in the basic nature of housing units and arrangements make direct comparisons very difficult. Far more respondents in both sites have access to household technology than in the 1960s. While car ownership in Pskov rose sharply from 2 percent to 20 percent, it remained over 90 percent in Jackson; ownership of two-wheel vehicles remained basically unchanged in Pskov. Proportions having a television set in Pskov rose from 49 percent to 98 percent in 1986, and 42 percent now have color sets; in Jackson overall set ownership was already at 97 percent in 1965, but by 1986 89 percent of Jackson respondents now had a color set (vs. less than 5 percent in 1965). Proportions having radios remained at well over 90 percent in both countries, although the 1986 proportions having stereo components had reached 65 percent in Jackson and 16 percent in Pskov. The proportions having more than 100 books in the household rose from 23 percent to 38 percent in Jackson and from 14 percent to 41 percent in Pskov. Telephone access rose from 90 percent to 96 percent in Jackson and from 11 percent to 23 percent in Pskov; access to some type of garden increased from 25 percent to 37 percent in Pskov and was at 48 percent in Jackson.

In general, then, the two sites showed parallel shifts in the greater number of more educated persons, in smaller households, in having fewer children, and in having greater access to household technology (particularly communications technology). The 1965 and 1986 Pskov and Jackson samples were more homogeneous with regard to distance from their city centers because of the Jackson sampling frame. Far more Jackson respondents were also unmarried in 1986 than in 1965, and far more than in Pskov, making this one of the major characteristics by which residents of the two sites differ from one another.

Time Use

There are several similarities in the time-use trends in Pskov and Jackson between 1965 and 1986. These include:

- Somewhat more housework done by employed men, and a considerable decline in the housework done by both employed and non-employed women;
- Relatively more time devoted to children, particularly on a per child basis;
- Gains in free time, particularly for women;
- Significant gains in time spent watching television, almost equal to the gains in free time; and,
- Significant declines in time spent on media activities that compete with television, namely reading, radio listening and movie attendance. In Pskov, there was also a significant decline in the time spent in educational activities.

While visiting time was slightly higher in Pskov (mainly among non-employed women), such social time in Jackson declined considerably over the 20-year period.

Work

In general, then, one is struck first by the smaller changes in time use shown in the Soviet data in comparison to some rather significant shifts in the American data. A large part of the shift in the Jackson data is, of course, due to the increased proportion of women who are working. At the same time, however, there is a small decrease in the work times of men in Jackson, a decline which is more apparent in the national trend data (where it is found among women who are employed as well). To a large extent, these declines tend to offset some of the overall increased work times brought about by women's increased participation in the labor force.

There is also some decline in Pskov in actual work time, although that is entirely due to the increasing proportions of men and women who are not employed (because of early retirement, maternity leave, and the like). However, the working times among workers are remarkably stable, if not virtually identical, between 1965 and 1986 in Pskov.

Housework

Perhaps the major time change over the two decades occurs for women and the decreased time they spend doing housework and family care activities. This shift is clear in both societies and among both employed and non-employed women. It is found in virtually all core housework activities: cooking, cleaning, laundry, and other housekeeping. In the U.S. data, this decline has been accompanied by a parallel increase in the housework times of men; that increase is not found in the Soviet data.

To some extent, this decline is reflected in decreased shopping time in the Soviet and American data, but this activity has not been affected as much. This is probably due to the increased shopping for clothing and other durable goods, rather than for grocery shopping. (See the next chapter.)

Nor does the decrease carry over to child care, especially among non-employed Soviet women. Many more of them are able to spend more time in child care, particularly if they are on maternity leave. Among American non-employed women, on the other hand, child-care time is down from 1965 levels, but these women also have fewer children to care for than they did at that time.

There are clearer, contrasting trends regarding travel time—outside of the commute to work which has remained rather constant across time. But while Pskov citizens are spending slightly less time in such travel, in the American samples more transit time is spent for family, personal and other reasons, especially among employed women.

Personal Needs

Again time spent on personal needs has remained quite similar over time in Pskov. Basically, sleeping, eating, and grooming time has not changed over the 20-year period. Pskov residents spend somewhat more time resting than previously, however.

Sleeping times in Jackson, in contrast, are down from 1965 levels, although only by about an hour per week. Time spent eating is also down, as is time spent resting. The one personal care activity to show an increase is time spent on personal hygiene and grooming, which has risen more than 10 percent over the two decades; this increase is also found in the national sample.

Free Time

Free time has increased in both countries. However, in both countries the free time of women has gained more than men. The gains were also greater (seven to 12 hours per week) among non-employed women in both Pskov and Jackson. Among Jackson's employed men, free time was actually down slightly.

The major recipient, and possibly a cause, of this increase was television. Television time has almost doubled in Pskov since 1965 and is up three to eight hours per week in Jackson. Yet different processes are involved in the two countries, since television was already at saturation levels in Jackson in 1965. Thus, it has been improvements in technology (color sets, longer broadcast days, more channels, etc.) that seem related to increased viewing in the United States (Robinson 1981), while in the Soviet Union most of the increase can be attributed to the fact that unlike today, about half of the Pskov population did not own a television in 1965.

One result has been a slight decrease in time spent reading in the two countries, and some decline in time spent attending movies and listening to the radio as a primary activity in Pskov. The major U.S. decrease, however, is found in social life—especially for employed men and women. In the Soviet case, social time and interaction have increased markedly—particularly among women. Educational time in Pskov, on the other hand, has decreased markedly. This may in some way be linked to the increased time watching television, much more of which is of an educational nature in the Soviet Union.

6

Subjective Aspects of Daily Life

Of the several hundred attitude and expectation questions in the survey, we have selected a few for initial differences and interpretation. These were chosen to illustrate the range of content in the questionnaire, which varies from work and housework questions on the one hand, to questions on free time and general levels of satisfaction on the other. These are examined in Tables 6.1 to 6.6 for Pskov and Tables 6.7 to 6.12 for Jackson. Each table refers to separate content areas in the questionnaire.

Pskov Responses

Work

Table 6.1 examines five major questions about work involvement and satisfaction. First it can be seen that 42 percent of the Pskov sample who worked said they were "completely" devoted to their work, while another 24 percent said they were sometimes greatly involved and sometimes indifferent. Some 28 percent said they were not particularly involved, and 2 percent said they actually would prefer not to work at all. There were not large differences between men and women in response to this question, although men (45 percent) were slightly more likely to say they were completely involved than were women (40 percent).

More than half of all employed men and women (58 percent) felt they *almost always* worked to the full extent of their abilities, and 33 percent of employed men and women said they worked this hard most of the time. At the other end of the scale, 8 percent of employed men vs. 6 percent of employed women felt they only sometimes or almost never worked to their fullest capacity. While 62 percent of women said they almost always worked to their fullest capabilities most of the time compared to only 54 percent of men who said they worked that hard, 35 percent of employed men (30 percent of employed women) said they worked to their fullest capabilities most of the time.

In terms of general satisfaction with work conditions, there were again some small differences by gender. Only 13 percent of employed men and women said they were partially dissatisfied with their work hours, with 61 percent of employed men and 54 percent of employed women saying they

Table 6.1
Responses by Pskov Respondents to Subjective Question about Work

	Men	Women	Total
W6. How involved are you in your main work?			
1. I devote myself completely to my work	45	40	42
2. Sometimes I am greatly involved in my work; sometimes I am indifferent	23	25	24
3. I work as much as is demanded and do not feel any particular involvement	27	29	28
4. If it were possible, I would prefer not to work	1	3	2
8. Hard to say	<u>4</u>	<u>4</u>	<u>4</u>
	100	100	100
W13. Do you work to the full extent of your abilities?			
1. Almost always	54	62	58
2. Most of the time	35	30	33
3. Some of the time	7	5	6
4. Almost never	1	1	1
8. Hard to say	<u>3</u>	<u>1</u>	<u>1</u>
	100	100	100
W19. To what extent are you satisfied or dissatisfied with the following aspects of your job?			
A. Length of the workweek			
1. Completely dissatisfied	7	8	8
2. More dissatisfied than satisfied	4	6	5
3. Partly satisfied, partly not	13	15	14
4. More satisfied than not	16	17	16
5. Completely satisfied	<u>61</u>	<u>54</u>	<u>57</u>
	100	100	100
B. Your job as a whole			
1. Completely dissatisfied	5	5	5
2. More dissatisfied than satisfied	5	4	5
3. Partly satisfied, partly not	20	24	22
4. More satisfied than not	29	32	30
5. Completely satisfied	<u>40</u>	<u>36</u>	<u>38</u>
	100	100	100
W27. How much do you like or dislike working (on your main job)?			
1. Dislike very much	2	2	2
2. Dislike more than like	6	7	7
3. Equally dislike and like	27	31	29
4. Like more than dislike	41	40	40
5. Like very much	<u>25</u>	<u>20</u>	<u>22</u>
	100	100	100

were "completely" satisfied. And 40 percent of employed men and 36 percent of employed women said they were completely satisfied with their job as a whole. A lower proportion (22 percent) said they liked their jobs very much, again higher among men (25 percent) than among women (20 percent); less than 10 percent of employed people in Pskov said they didn't like their jobs.

Housework

The figures in Table 6.2 show that 35 percent of the employed men and 52 percent of the employed women in Pskov said they liked doing housework. In numerical terms, while paid work was rated about 3.7 on average by both men and women (on a scale from 1 = Dislike a great deal to 5 = Like a great deal), housework in general was rated 3.6 by women and 3.3 by men.

There was wide variation in the ratings of liking to do household tasks in regard to the specific task involved. Thus, caring for children was the most liked activity for both men (43 percent) and women (55 percent), while knitting and various clothing-care activities were the least liked household tasks for men (0–9 percent);repairing appliances was the least liked task for women (3–5 percent). Among the more enjoyable household activities for men were repairing appliances (53 percent), gardening (29 percent), cooking (27 percent) and making house repairs (26 percent).

Women tended to like these latter two tasks slightly less than men did. Generally small differences were found between labor-force and non-labor-force women in liking these tasks, although employed women were slightly more likely to say they enjoyed mending and knitting than were non-employed women.

At the same time, the clothing care tasks of mending and cleaning clothing were among the household tasks all women liked least—along with shopping for groceries. In general, employed women did not evaluate doing many of these activities much differently than did non-employed women. Women and men differed much less on liking grocery shopping than on liking clothes shopping, which 51 percent of women liked compared to 19 percent of men.

Not surprisingly, women felt much more skilled in housework tasks than did men. More than 90 percent of women, both employed and non-employed, said they had at least basic skills in cooking, cleaning and clothes-care skills; and the figures in the second half of Table 6.2 show nearly two-thirds of the women rated their cooking skills as "good" or "excellent," as compared to the less than 30 percent of men who responded similarly. Women also rated their cleaning skills much higher than men.

In addition, women rated their sewing and knitting skills much higher

Table 6.2
Housework Attitudes and Abilities in Pskov

| | Men | | Women | | |
	Not Employed	Employed	Not Employed	Employed	Total

H1. Listed below are several kinds of activities which you may do at home. Keep in mind that we are interested in learning to what extent you like to do something, and not whether it's important to you or what you get out of completing the activity.

To what extent do you like to or dislike to . . .
(% Who Like)

	Not Employed (Men)	Employed (Men)	Not Employed (Women)	Employed (Women)	Total
1. Cook	25	27	49	49	39
2. Clean house (sweep, mop floor, etc.)	17	15	50	50	35
3. Wash and iron clothes	8	4	39	40	25
4. Mend clothes	6	9	22	30	16
5. Sew clothes	3	4	36	39	22
6. Knitting	1	0	53	56	31
7. Repair appliances and household gadgets	57	52	5	3	27
8. Make repairs in the house (apartment)	38	24	21	26	28
9. Preserve (fruits, vegetables, etc.)	23	14	60	52	43
10. Gardening	32	29	27	25	29
11. Take care and bring up children	52	45	61	51	50
12. Grocery shopping	26	16	28	31	17
13. Shopping for clothes, shoes, etc.	26	17	50	51	27
14. To what extent do you like housework, on the whole?	17	35	50	52	44

Table 6.2—continued

H6. Would you evaluate your ability to do the following household chores?
(% Good or Excellent)

1. Cook	32	28	67	66	52
2. Clean house (sweep, mop floor, etc.)	46	44	84	82	67
3. Wash and iron clothes	26	23	84	80	58
4. Mend clothes	13	14	56	56	37
5. Sew clothes	2	0	26	29	16
6. Knitting	1	0	35	35	20
7. Repair appliances and household gadgets	44	41	3	1	20
8. Carpentry	32	22	1	*	14
9. Repair house (apartment)	50	36	30	27	38
10. Preserve vegetables, fruits, etc.	23	13	57	52	41
11. Gardening	28	31	25	27	27
12. Repair of cars, motorcycles, etc.	37	29	1	1	16

than did their male counterparts. Conversely, men were much more skilled in repairing appliances (more than 40 percent good or excellent vs. only 1 percent for women), doing home repairs (39 percent vs. 27 percent), repairing motor vehicles (31 percent to 1 percent) and doing carpentry (24 percent to 1 percent) than were women; many other men rated themselves as having at least some skills in these areas, even at the "fair" or "poor" levels.

Men and women perceived their gardening skills much more equally, although men were slightly higher here than women (31 percent vs. 27 percent). Generally, employed men reported slightly lower levels of household skills than non-employed men. It was similarly the case that non-employed women reported slightly higher skill levels than did employed women.

Leisure Skills and Preferences

As shown in Table 6.3, men and women in Pskov felt most skilled in the leisure skills of playing checkers/dominoes (28 percent "good" or "excellent"), dancing (16 percent), knitting (20 percent), and playing cards (20 percent). Women rated their flower-growing skills higher than did men and also their skills in knitting, dancing, and singing. Men rated their skills in playing chess, playing billiards, playing cards, playing checkers/dominoes, technical/scientific hobbies and photography notably higher than did women.

Lowest skill levels were reported in playing musical instruments, in creative writing of prose and poetry, and in collecting things. A slightly higher proportion of men (5 percent) reported being able to play a musical instrument at a good or excellent level than did women (2 percent).

Pskov residents enjoyed spending their free time in a wide variety of locations, particularly at the circus (which is not a permanent facility but one which comes in touring companies), at libraries, and at indoor gymnasiums. Women enjoyed being in concert halls and stage theaters more than men; men preferred spending time in game rooms and indoor gyms. There were few systematic differences by employment status among either men or women in these enjoyment ratings for different leisure facilities.

Free Time

As shown in Table 6.4, men and women in Pskov feel they are more likely to plan their free time activities ahead of time than not to plan ahead, and by about a two-to-one margin. The largest group (34 percent) say they sometimes plan ahead and sometimes not. There are few systematic or significant differences in planning ahead by sex; however, employed men and women are more likely to plan ahead than are non-employed men and women.

Women are less likely than men to be satisfied both with the amount of free time they have (34 percent) and with how they spend that free time (29 percent); this is more true for employed women than for non-employed women. In contrast, 53 percent of of employed men are satisfied with the amount of free time they have and 49 percent with how they spend that free time. Non-employed men and women are above average in satisfaction with the *amount* of free time they have, but only about average in satisfaction with how they spend that free time. Women in Pskov are also more likely to feel a lack of free time more than men. Thus, 34 percent of employed women and 23 percent of non-employed women said they constantly feel a lack of free time compared to only 21 percent of employed men. For both men and women, then, the employed feel more such time pressure than do the non-employed.

Finally, with regard to whether people in Pskov get more satisfaction from their work than from their free time activities, the answers are mixed. More workers say that free-time activities (22 percent) give them greater satisfaction than work activities (17 percent), but most say they get equal satisfaction from both types of activities. Employed women are more

Table 6.3
Leisure Skills as Rated in Pskov

	MEN		WOMEN		
	Not Employed	Employed	Not Employed	Employed	TOTAL

I3. "How would you rate your leisure time skills and interests?"
(% Good or Excellent)

	Not Employed (Men)	Employed (Men)	Not Employed (Women)	Employed (Women)	TOTAL
1. Draw, sculpt, carve, etc.	12	6	9	5	6
2. Knit, embroider	0	1	33	36	20
3. Play musical instruments	6	5	4	2	4
4. Sing	8	7	14	13	11
5. Dance	8	11	21	21	16
6. Grow flowers	6	5	21	21	14
7. Collect things	3	4	6	5	4
8. Photography, movies	17	14	4	3	8
9. Write poetry, prose	0	1	1	1	1
10. Play chess	15	17	1	2	8
11. Play checkers, dominoes	32	36	22	21	28
12. Play pool, billiards	11	19	1	1	8
13. Play cards	30	29	16	13	20
14. Technical, scientific hobbies	18	16	1	1	7
15. Take care of pets	20	17	18	19	18

likely to say they get greater satisfaction from free-time activities (25 percent) than are men (14 percent).

Social Contacts

An idea about whom the residents of Pskov spend their free time with can be obtained from the answers to Question I2 in the questionnaire. The most frequent contacts are of course within the family. As shown in Table 6.5, some 70 percent of respondents said they spend leisure time with either their spouse or children (or both) "almost every day." The proportion is equally high among men and women, although higher among men who are employed than men who are not employed.

Table 6.3—continued

II4. To what extent do you like to spend your free time at (% who like)

1. Movie houses	69	72	76	75	74
2. Other theaters	48	51	59	62	57
3. Museums	55	53	56	54	54
4. Concert halls	8	9	11	13	11
5. The circus	43	43	41	40	41
6. Libraries	49	51	49	48	49
7. Places of culture	29	27	23	22	24
8. Hobby clubs; amateur group	9	7	5	3	5
9. Discotheque, dancing	15	14	13	12	13
10. Game room (cards, chess, etc.)	16	16	4	3	9
11. Indoor gyms, stadiums	24	25	14	12	18
12. Swimming pools—indoor	14	13	9	8	10
13. Cafes, bars	25	27	15	14	20
14. Restaurants	20	19	13	12	15
15. Places of culture in general	57	57	59	55	56

The second most frequent types of social partners for free-time activities are one's parents. About one-fifth of Pskov respondents (20 percent) say they spent free time with their parents almost every day. Here the proportions are highest among non-employed men and women. This is probably due in large part to the higher proportion of such respondents who live with or near their parents.

The next most frequent social partners for free-time activities are neighbors, with whom 8 percent of respondents say they spend time almost every day. The proportion is again slightly higher among non-employed respondents than the employed. The same pattern holds for contacts with friends outside the neighborhood, and with one's brothers and sisters. However, the estimated daily contact rate for friends is only 3 percent and for siblings only 2 percent.

The final group on the list of partners for free-time activities, namely relatives, were described as everyday contacts by 5 percent of Pskov

Table 6.4
Responses of Pskov Respondents to Subjective Questions about Free Time
(of those expressing an opinion)

	MEN		WOMEN		
	Not Employed	Employed	Not Employed	Employed	Total

I26. Some people plan their use of free time out in advance. Others wait until they have free time and only then think about what to do with it. How is it with you?

	Not Employed	Employed	Not Employed	Employed	Total
1. Almost always plan ahead	8	18	16	18	17
2. Most of the time plan ahead	25	27	23	29	27
3. Sometimes plan ahead, sometimes not	33	35	30	34	34
4. Most of the time don't plan ahead	14	9	9	9	9
5. Almost always don't plan ahead	20	11	22	10	12
	100%	100%	100%	100%	100%

I27. Please indicate how much you are satisfied with the amount of free time you have?

	Not Employed	Employed	Not Employed	Employed	Total
1. Completely satisfied	31	20	15	9	16
2. Basically satisfied	27	33	21	25	28
3. Partly satisfied, partly not	13	20	21	21	20
4. Not very satisfied	19	18	21	29	23
5. Completely dissatisfied	10	9	22	16	13
	100%	100%	100%	100%	100%

.............with how you spend your free time

	Not Employed	Employed	Not Employed	Employed	Total
1. Completely satisfied	19	13	11	6	10
2. Basically satisfied	35	36	24	23	29
3. Partly satisfied, partly not	20	26	23	28	27
4. Not very satisfied	12	20	24	31	25
5. Completely dissatisfied	13	6	13	11	9
	100%	100%	100%	100%	100%

Table 6.4—continued

I30. Some people never have enough free time, other people have nothing better to occupy themselves with free time. What do you experience, an excess or lack of free time?					
1. Constantly feel excess free time	6	2	3	1	2
2. Sometimes feel excess time	14	7	5	6	7
3. Feel neither excess nor lack of free time	47	37	38	26	32
4. Sometimes feel lack of free time	19	32	31	32	32
5. Constantly feel lack of free time	<u>13</u>	<u>21</u>	<u>23</u>	<u>34</u>	<u>28</u>
	100%	100%	100%	100%	100%

I34. Work and free time are two important areas of a person's life. Which do you get more satisfaction from?					
1. I get more satisfaction from work	NA	19	NA	14	17
2. I get more satisfaction from free time activities	NA	14	NA	25	22
3. I get about the same amount of satisfaction from work as from free time activities	<u>NA</u>	<u>62</u>	<u>NA</u>	<u>61</u>	<u>61</u>
	NA	100%	NA	100%	100%

respondents. Women, especially non-employed women, were more likely to say they got together with relatives almost every day than were men. The differences between men and women are not as great here as are the variations by age with whom people spend their free time.

Media Preferences

The most popular and frequent form of at-home, free-time activities are looking at TV and reading; among the younger adults (age 18–29) and

Table 6.5
Differences in Extent of Social Contact during Free Time Activities

I2: "With Whom Do You Usually Spend Leisure Time in the Evenings?"

Proportion (%) Saying Almost Every Day	Men		Women		
	Not Employed	Employed	Not Employed	Employed	Total
1) Your neighbors	8	5	11	9	8
2) Friends (who are not neighbors)	12	2	7	2	3
3) Your parents	23	15	30	21	20
4) Brothers or sisters living separately	2	2	2	2	2
5) Spouse and/or children	56	73	68	69	70
6) Relatives	2	4	9	6	5

among women aged 18–39, listening to music records is also a popular activity. The level of interest is rather high for all types of TV programs. Interest in informational programs, such as "Time," national news broadcasts, "Novosti," "Studio 9," broadcasts on problems of economy and "Man and the Law," increases with age. At the same time, interest in musical-variety programs decreases with age among men, but increases with age among women. Feature films, sports broadcasts, programs for youth, and promotional broadcasts are least liked among all age groups.

Reading preferences among men and women are quite different. Whereas the three most popular genres among younger men are detective stories, adventure stories and historical novels, women's favorites include detective stories, novels about the contemporary world and books about cooking and housekeeping. These differences are less apparent among the older age groups, where interest in books about war are highest among both men and women.

Musical preferences also vary significantly by sex and by age, as shown in Table 6.6. As a rule, one finds higher proportions of people among older age cohorts who like to listen to a variety of music. The main exceptions are for variety and rock music, and, to a lesser extent, jazz. In the case of rock music, one can see that less than 5 percent of those aged 60–65 like this type of music, compared to the nearly 50 percent of those in the 18–24 age group who report liking it.

On the other hand, less than a third of those aged 18–24 like folk music compared to almost 80 percent of those aged 60–65. This generation gap in music preferences is almost as wide for revolutionary songs and anthems, for lyrical and romantic music, and for string orchestra music.

There are also some marked differences in music preferences by gender. Both older and younger women say they like opera and symphony music more than men. Men, on the other hand, state more of a clear preference for rock music.

Jackson Responses

Work

Table 6.7 examines the same questions about work as Table 6.1. First it can be seen that 38 percent of the Jackson sample who worked said they

Table 6.6
Music Preference Differences by Age in Pskov

I12: "What Kinds of Music Do You Like to Listen to?"

Types of music		Men		Women	
Age:	18-24	60-65	18-24	60-65
Opera	3	5	8	18
Classical	1	3	12	8
Folk music	19	84	42	72
Revolutionary and popular	3	48	14	47
Music for string orchestra	3	19	7	14
Lyrical songs and romances	32	67	45	67
Operetta	18	30	42	42
Variety	90	49	97	45
Jazz	23	16	21	9
Rock	61	5	36	2

Table 6.7
Responses by Jackson Respondents to Subjective Questions about Work

	Men	Women	Total
W6. How involved are you in your main work:			
1. I devote myself completely to my work	40	36	38
2. Sometimes I am greatly involved in my work, sometimes I am different	48	51	49
3. I work as much as is demanded and do not feel any particular involvement	5	7	6
4. If it were possible, I would prefer not to work	4	4	4
5. Hard to say	<u>3</u>	<u>2</u>	<u>2</u>
	100%	100%	100%
W13. Do you work to the full extent of your abilities?			
1. Almost always	39	51	44
2. Most of the time	46	40	43
3. Some of the time	12	7	10
4. Almost never	2	1	2
5. Hard to say	<u>1</u>	<u>1</u>	<u>1</u>
	100%	100%	100%

W19. To what extent are you satisfied or dissatisfied with the following aspects of your job?

A. Length of the workweek	Men	Women	Total
1. Completely dissatisfied	6	3	5
2. More dissatisfied than satisfied	6	4	5
3. Partly satisfied, partly not	13	18	15
4. More satisfied than not	35	34	35
5. Completely satisfied	<u>40</u>	<u>41</u>	<u>40</u>
	100%	100%	100%
B. Your job as a whole			
1. Completely dissatisfied	3	3	3
2. More dissatisfied than satisfied	7	7	7
3. Partly satisfied, partly not	19	21	20
4. More satisfied than not	47	39	43
5. Completely satisfied	<u>24</u>	<u>29</u>	<u>26</u>
	100%	100%	100%

W27. How much do you like or dislike working (on your main job)?	Men	Women	Total
1. Dislike very much	4	2	3
2. Dislike more than like	6	5	5
3. Equally dislike and like	18	18	18
4. Like more than dislike	38	40	39
5. Like very much	<u>35</u>	<u>35</u>	<u>25</u>
	100%	100%	100%

were "completely" devoted to their work, while another 49 percent said they were sometimes greatly involved and sometimes indifferent. Only 10 percent said they either were not particularly involved or feel they actually would prefer not to work. There were very few differences between men and women in response to this question.

There were larger gender differences in the question concerning how hard employed men worked. While more than half of the women (51 percent) felt they "almost always" worked to the full extent of their abilities, only 39 percent of employed men felt they worked that hard. Some 14 percent of employed men vs. 8 percent of employed women felt they only "sometimes" or "almost never" worked to their fullest capacity.

In terms of overall satisfaction with work, however, there were again no major differences by gender. Only 10 percent of employed men and women said they were dissatisfied with their work hours, with 40 percent of both employed men and women saying they were "completely" satisfied. And almost a quarter (24 percent men and 29 percent women) said they were completely satisfied with their job as a whole. A higher proportion of both men and women—35 percent—said they liked their jobs very much, and less than 10 percent said they didn't like their jobs.

Housework

In contrast, only about a quarter of men and women said they liked to do housework in general; as seen in Table 6.8, the figure for women (housewives) was higher (32 percent). The overall ratings on a scale of 1 (Dislike very much) to 5 (Like very much) scale were 3.2 for women and 2.8 for men, being below the 3.0 midpoint or on the dislike side of the scale.

Of the various tasks associated with housework, three were clearly rated most positively: cooking (55 percent like), raising children (51 percent like) and gardening (41 percent like). Women tended to like these tasks more than men, but not by large margins for cooking and gardening. While there are usually not large differences between labor-force and non-labor-force women in liking these tasks, labor-force women are slightly more likely to say they like doing them.

At the other end of the scale, three clothes care tasks (mending, sewing and cleaning) were liked by fewer respondents (7 percent to 16 percent) along with various aspects of cleaning the house. Employed men especially did not like doing any of these clothes or cleaning tasks (0 percent to 20 percent). Women and men differed much less on liking grocery shopping than on liking clothes shopping, which more than 60 percent of women liked compared to less than 30 percent of men.

Jackson women felt much more skilled in doing housework tasks than men. More than 80 percent of women, both employed and non-employed,

Table 6.8
Housework Attitudes and Abilities in Jackson

	Men		Women		
	Not Employed	Employed	Not Employed	Employed	Total

H1. To what extent do you like to or dislike to . . . (on a scale from 1=Dislike a great deal to 5=Like a great deal)
(% Who Like)

	Not Employed	Employed	Not Employed	Employed	Total
1. Cook	47	53	54	59	55
2. Clean house (sweep, mop floor, etc.)	22	14	23	25	20
3. Wash and iron clothes	20	7	19	23	16
4. Mend clothes	0	3	9	11	7
5. Sew clothes	0	4	24	24	15
6. Knitting	0	5	20	24	15
7. Repair appliances and household gadgets	58	53	11	8	29
8. Make repairs in the house (apartment)	55	50	19	31	46
9. Preserve (fruits, vegetables, etc.)	8	13	31	30	22
10. Gardening	39	40	43	43	41
11. Take care and bring up children	24	43	58	60	51
12. Grocery shopping	33	37	43	44	41
13. Shopping for clothes, shoes, etc.	28	26	57	65	46
14. To what extent do you like housework, on the whole?	24	18	32	32	26

again rated their cooking, cleaning and clothes care skills as good or excellent compared to only between 45 percent to 62 percent of men. Men, on the other hand, reported being much more skilled than women in repairing appliances, houses and cars—and doing carpentry work—than did women; still, only about 60 percent of men rated their skills in this area

Table 6.8—continued

H6. Would you evaluate your ability to do the following household chores?
(% Good or Excellent)

1. Cook	62	62	88	81	70
2. Clean house (sweep, mop floor, etc.)	61	61	79	86	69
3. Wash and iron clothes	55	45	85	88	64
4. Mend clothes	21	13	50	48	31
5. Sew clothes	9	9	45	40	25
6. Knitting	13	8	26	27	17
7. Repair appliances and household gadgets	60	56	13	9	29
8. Carpentry	53	54	13	6	26
9. Repair house (apartment)	56	60	18	13	31
10. Preserve (vegetables, fruits, etc.)	21	20	37	33	26
11. Gardening	47	42	45	34	37
12. Repair of cars, motorcycles, etc.	39	44	7	6	20

as good or excellent. Men and women were much more even in gardening skills, with about 40 percent of each claiming good or excellent skills.

Leisure Skills and Preferences

As shown in Table 6.9, Jackson men and women felt most skilled in the leisure areas of reading (69 percent "good" or "excellent"), taking care of pets (58 percent), and playing cards (50 percent). Women rated their reading skills higher than did men and also their skills in needlework, dancing and taking care of pets. Men rated their skills in playing chess, playing pool, and technical/scientific hobbies higher than women rated these same skills. Lowest skills were reported in playing musical instruments, in creative writing of prose and poetry, in the visual arts and in playing chess.

Jackson residents enjoyed spending their free time in a wide variety of locations, particularly in restaurants (91 percent like), indoor sports facili-

Table 6.9
Leisure Skills as Rated in Jackson

| | Men | | Women | | |
	Not Employed	Employed	Not Employed	Employed	Total

I3.To what extent do you rate your leisure time and interests?"
(% Good or Excellent)

	Not Employed	Employed	Not Employed	Employed	Total
1. Draw, sculpt, carve,etc.	12	7	11	11	11
2. Knit, embroider	1	8	25	33	16
3. Play musical instruments	8	10	11	8	9
4. Sing	13	18	21	22	18
5. Dance	21	13	32	30	26
6. Grow flowers	24	36	37	39	32
7. Collect things	25	20	29	33	28
8. Photography, movies	25	15	20	24	23
9. Write poetry, prose	6	18	7	6	7
10. Play chess	21	13	6	5	13
11. Play checkers, dominoes	34	33	25	20	28
12. Playing pool and billiards	36	32	13	10	23
13. Play cards	53	49	49	46	50
14. Technical, scientific hobbies	30	24	12	6	17
15. Take care of pets	53	47	60	67	58
16. Reading	58	53	89	78	69

ties (62 percent) and movie houses (59 percent). More women than men enjoyed spending time in churches, restaurants, places for dancing, places for culture, libraries and stage theatres; men preferred spending time in game rooms and indoor gyms more often than did women. Employed people tended to report liking being in those places less than non-employed people.

Free Time

As shown in Table 6.10, men and women in Jackson feel they are more likely to plan their free-time activities ahead of time (39 percent) than not

Table 6.9—continued

II4. To what extent do you like to spend your free time at . . .
   (4 or 5 on scale from 1=Dislike a great deal to 5=Like a great deal)

1. Movie houses	55	62	62	62	59
2. Other theaters	43	32	62	54	53
3. Museums	59	60	60	51	58
4. Concert halls	50	37	57	65	52
5. The circus	48	56	57	65	53
6. Libraries	48	33	57	63	53
7. Places of culture	44	27	56	63	53
8. Hobby clubs; amateur group	35	49	28	36	35
9. Discotheque, dancing	42	45	58	52	44
10. Game room (cards, chess, etc.)	40	61	25	57	35
11. Indoor gyms, stadium	66	77	58	56	60
12. Swimming pools--indoor	66	77	65	65	62
13. Cafes, bars	56	70	54	56	54
14. Restaurants	75	35	89	81	91
15. Places of leisure	58	41	71	60	62
16. Churches	34	42	59	62	52

---

to plan ahead (18 percent) and by a fairly large margin. However, the largest group (42 percent) say they sometimes plan ahead and sometimes not. There are few systematic or significant differences in planning ahead by sex or by employment status.

Employed women are least likely to be satisfied both with the amount of free time they have (33 percent) and with how they spend that free time (33 percent). In contrast, 53 percent of employed men are satisfied with how they spend that free time. Non-employed men and women are above average in satisfaction with the amount of free time they have, but only about average in satisfaction with how they spend that free time.

With regard to feelings of having too much or too little free time, not surprisingly, major differences are found by employment status. Some 69 percent of employed women at least sometimes have feelings of a lack of

Table 6.10
Responses of Jackson Respondents to Subjective Questions about Free Time

	Men		Women		
	Not Employed	Employed	Not Employed	Employed	Total

I26. Some people plan their use of free time out in advance. Others wait until they have free time and only then think about what to do with it. How is it with you?

	Not Employed	Employed	Not Employed	Employed	Total
1. Almost always plan ahead	19	9	10	13	12
2. Most of the time plan ahead	29	29	23	29	27
3. Sometimes plan ahead, sometimes not	33	44	42	44	42
4. Most of the time don't plan ahead	14	12	12	9	11
5. Almost always don't plan ahead	6	7	10	5	<u>7</u> 100%

I27. Please indicate how much you are satisifed with the amount of free time you have?

	Not Employed	Employed	Not Employed	Employed	Total
1. Completely satisfied	46	8	24	8	16
2. Basically satisfied	27	39	36	25	33
3. Partly satisfied, partly not	18	28	23	33	27
4. Not very satisfied	4	21	9	27	17
5. Completely dissatisfied	5	4	8	7	<u>6</u> 100%

...with how you spend your free time

	Not Employed	Employed	Not Employed	Employed	Total
1. Completely satisfied	38	8	14	5	13
2. Basically satisfied	34	45	33	28	35
3. Partly satisfied, partly not	18	30	30	46	33
4. Not very satisfied	6	13	14	17	13
5. Completely dissatisfied	4	4	8	3	<u>5</u> 100%

Table 6.10—continued

I30. Some people never have enough free time, other people have nothing better to occupy themselves with free time. What do you experience, an excess or lack of free time?

1. Constantly feel excess free time	22	1	7	1	6
2. Sometimes feel excess time	13	15	21	14	16
3. Feel neither excess nor lack of free time	35	26	36	15	28
4. Sometimes feel lack of free time	20	43	27	43	36
5. Constantly feel lack of free time	10	14	8	26	<u>15</u> 100%

I23. Work and free time are two important areas of a person's life. Which do you get more satisfaction from?

1. I get more satisfaction from work	NA	12	NA	16	14
2. I get more satisfaction from free time activities	NA	31	NA	27	29
3. I get about the same amount of satisfaction	NA	56	NA	57	<u>57</u> 100%

free time an compared to only 35 percent of non-employed women; 57 percent of employed men at least sometimes feel a lack of free time compared to only 30 percent of non-employed men. In contrast, only 1 percent of employed men and women said they "constantly" have excess time compared to 7 percent of non-employed women and 22 percent of non-employed men.

Finally, Table 6.10 shows that more than half (57 percent) of both employed men and women said they get about equal satisfaction from their work activities and their free-time activities. While more people did say they get more satisfaction from free-time activities (29 percent) than from work activities (14 percent), the differences are not overwhelming. Both facets of life are clearly important for workers in Jackson.

Social Contacts

Outside of contacts with one's immediate family members, Table 6.11 shows that less than 5 percent of the Jackson respondents said they were in contact with other types of social partners during free time "almost every day." Women reported slightly higher contact rates than men and the non-employed slightly higher rates than the employed.

In addition to the 3 percent who reported daily contact with neighbors in Table 6.11, another 9 percent reported contact once or twice a week. These overall rates were about equal for all four sex-employment categories. More than one-third of the respondents (higher among the employed) said they "never" spent free time with neighbors.

Weekly contact with friends also involved an additional 13 percent of Jackson respondents, as compared to the 3 percent daily rate shown in Table 6.11. Again the rates were not much different by sex or employment status. Less than 10 percent of all Jackson respondents said they "never" spent leisure time in the evenings with friends.

Weekly contact with parents involved an additional 15 percent of Jackson respondents, as compared to the 4 percent daily rate shown in Table 6.11—again not much difference is seen by sex or employment status.

Table 6.11
Differences in Extent of Social Contact During Free Time Activities

	Men		Women		
	Not Employed	Employed	Not Employed	Employed	Total
I2: "With Whom Do You Spend Time in the Evenings..."					
(% "Almost Every Day")					
1. Your neighbors	2	1	6	4	3%
2. Friends (who are (not neighbors)	3	2	4	2	3%
3. Your parents	12	4	3	3	4%
4. Brothers or sisters (living separately)	3	2	3	2	2%
5. Spouse and/or children	62	64	70	75	69%
6. Relatives	5	2	4	5	4%

Some 9 percent of employed respondents, compared to 29 percent of non-employed respondents, said they never spent free time with their parents.

The weekly contact rate for spouse and children raises the figures in Table 6.11 by ten points for employed respondents and by seven points for non-employed respondents. Consistent with Table 6.11, women report higher contact with immediate family members than do men. Less than 10 percent of respondents report "never" getting together with a spouse or child. That same rate holds true for those who never get together with relatives, as well.

Media Preferences

Some rather large differences in music preferences by age are shown in Table 6.12, and some smaller difference by gender are present. The main music genres preferred by older respondents are folk, choral, easy listening, show tunes and country/western music—the last being the most popular type of music of those presented to respondents.

On the other hand, rock music was most popular among younger people. Jazz and romantic and classical music were popular on a relatively equal basis among younger and older listeners. Jazz was liked more by men, and romantic music more by women.

Summary, Comparisons and Conclusions

One is again struck by the many similarities between the data from Pskov and from Jackson in this initial examination of Soviet and American differences in attitudes and perceived skill levels. This is true for the overall distribution of responses to each question—such as the proportions satisfied or having a particular skill or work characteristic. It is also true, however, for the differences between men and women, and between employed and non-employed people, in responding to these subjective questions.

Thus, in both countries, we find rather similar proportions of workers who said they devote themselves completely to their work or who like to garden or to look after their children, or who plan their free-time activities ahead of time, or who get equal satisfaction from work and free time. There are few relative differences between men and women in responding to these questions in the two survey sites.

Nonetheless, there are some intriguing differences in responses. Soviet respondents are more likely to say they are "completely" satisfied with their jobs than are American respondents, more of whom say they are satisfied but not completely satisfied. However, more American workers

Table 6.12
Music Preference Differences by Age in Jackson

"Which of These Types of Music Do you Like to Listen to?"

| | | Men | | | Women | |
Age:	18-24	25-59	60-65	18-24	25-59	60-65
Opera	10	6	5	2	6	27
Classical	21	29	18	23	27	34
Folk music	31	44	55	2	35	46
Choral music	7	15	36	6	17	40
Easy listening	36	59	77	56	72	66
Romantic songs	31	26	27	69	68	60
Show tunes	15	19	46	19	28	66
Popular	41	65	38	69	68	63
Jazz	49	44	27	27	38	46
Rock	87	52	5	88	60	20
Country/western	36	55	77	46	60	51

say they like their jobs "very much," in comparison to Soviet workers, a third of whom say they equally like and dislike their jobs. Soviet respondents are more likely to say they like doing clothing-related cleaning and mending than American respondents, but American respondents are more likely to say they like cooking and shopping (for both groceries and for clothes) than are Soviet respondents.

These are related, as well, to the skill levels that are required and have been acquired in the two countries. Differences in answers given by American and Soviet workers may be explained by greater social and job security in the Soviet Union. Perhaps that is why Soviet workers are more satisfied with the various aspects of their working life. To be satisfied, however, is not to say that one likes the situation, as research in the United States regarding the differences between happiness and satisfaction has shown. Interestingly, job satisfaction and liking the job are lower among women than among men in Pskov; no such gender differences are found in Jackson.

Further analysis of replies shows that while 96 percent of the working inhabitants of Pskov consider their workload very heavy or heavy, some 55 percent of respondents noted that up to 30 minutes or more of their workday is spent on matters not directly connected to their main job. Nor can their work schedule be said to be overly rigid, given that 60 percent of workers feel that it is not particularly difficult to request an hour or two of time off and that 13 percent of the working inhabitants of Pskov had requested time off to take care of various items of family and daily business in the course of the week preceding the survey.

A comparison of the other data from both Pskov and Jackson not analyzed earlier in this chapter shows certain differences in the opinions of working people about their workload. In contrast to the 24 percent of workers in Pskov who consider their workload to be heavy, the percentage in Jackson is 42 percent. Nonetheless, most workers in Jackson (78 percent), as in Pskov, had no difficulty in requesting time off, and the reasons were similar to those from workers in Pskov—illness of family members, repairs to the apartment, receipt of services, and the like. More than half of Jackson workers (56 percent), as in Pskov, spent more than half an hour per day in matters not directly connected with their basic job.

There *were* significant differences in the work philosophies between workers in the U.S.S.R. and the U.S. Whereas 87 percent of Pskov respondents replied that each worker must feel a moral responsibility both for the use of his or her working time and for that of the time of co-workers, in Jackson this percentage was only 45 percent. At the same time, 66 percent of the workers surveyed in Pskov felt that the use of working time for matters not connected with the basic job should not be allowed (vs. 34 percent who saw no objection to this if work assignments had been completed); in Jackson the corresponding figure was 61 percent. Thus, about one-third of the workers in both Pskov and Jackson had a relaxed attitude toward the use of working time for other matters if work requirements had been met. Blue-collar workers had a somewhat stricter attitude than white-collar workers toward the use of working time for other matters, as did older workers. Among 50-to 65-year-olds, only 19 percent considered it permissible to use working time for personal purposes, compared to 41 percent among the 18-to-29-year-olds (in Jackson the corresponding figures were 34 percent and 43 percent).

This is related to the degree of effort expended in the work process. Among those aged 18–29, only 47 percent almost always work to their fullest extent; among 30-to 49-year-olds, this figure is 61 percent and among 50-to 65-year-olds, 76 percent. There is indeed an inverse correlation between working to the fullest and the attitudes toward taking off working time. Thus, among Pskov workers who almost always work at the fullest extent, 77 percent consider taking time off not allowable. On the other hand, among those who work to the fullest only part of the time, only 32 percent felt that way. The same relationship between responses was also found in Jackson.

The degree of satisfaction with various aspects of the organization of working time is also connected with work intensity. Table 6.13 shows degrees of satisfaction a five-point scale, where 5 is the maximum rating and 1 is the minimum. The table shows that working people in Pskov are most satisfied with time-related aspects of work—the number of days off (4.2), the length of the lunch hour (4.1) and the length of the workweek (4.1). The least satisfactory are the need to work in different shifts (3.5), how well one's working time is used (3.7) and the commute to work (3.7). The most satisfactory to workers in Jackson are the length of the commute to work (4.0), the length of the workweek (4.0), the length of the lunch hour (4.0) and the time when work begins and ends (4.0). The least satisfactory are the need to work in different shifts (3.5), the amount of work (3.8) and the number of days off (3.8).

Table 6.13
Differences in Satisfaction with Various Aspects of Work
(on a scale from 1=Completely Dissatisfied to 5=Completely Satisfied)

	(n=)	Pskov (1853)	Jackson (440)
1. Length of the workweek		4.1	4.0
2. Amount of work to do		3.8	3.8
3. How well your work time is used		3.7	3.9
4. Number of days off		4.2	3.8
5. Time job starts and ends		4.0	4.0
6. Length of the lunch hour		4.1	4.0
7. Work different shifts		3.5	3.5
8. Time spent commuting to work		3.7	4.0
9. Your job on the whole		3.9	3.9

The figures again demonstrate the striking similarity between the degrees of satisfaction with various aspects of work life among employed people in Pskov and Jackson. While there are some differences (especially concerning the length of the work commute, where in Pskov it is one of the least satisfactory aspects and in Jackson the most satisfactory), the ratings of overall job satisfaction are the same (3.9) in both cities.

7

Summary and Conclusions

This volume has reviewed the history and results of the first joint study of objective and subjective living conditions in the United States and the Soviet Union. This first joint survey in the two countries took almost eight years to complete. Most of the preparatory work was negotiated during periods in the late 1970s and early 1980s during considerable international tension and diplomatic hostility. Nonetheless, the study resulted in an unprecedented exchange of comparable scientific data on the state of daily life and living conditions in the two countries. The study was carried out under the auspices of the U.S.-USSR Commission on the Humanities and Social Sciences of the American Council of Learned Societies and the USSR Academy of Sciences, administered in the United States by the International Research & Exchanges Board (IREX). The research was supported by grants from the Alfred P. Sloan Foundation, the National Science Foundation, the International Research & Exchanges Board, the Soviet Academy of Sciences and the University of Maryland. Extraordinary care and time was devoted to ensuring that question areas of social science interest in both countries were represented equally and that strict comparability of language and phrasing of the survey questions was achieved through back translation.

The Soviet study was conducted with 2,181 adults aged 18 to 65 in the city of Pskov (population 197,000), which is located in the northwest part of the Russian Republic roughly midway between Leningrad and Riga (Latvia). The American study was conducted with 710 adult residents of Jackson, Michigan, a community of about 80,000 located about eighty miles west of Detroit. In both sites, survey respondents kept a complete 24-hour diary of all their daily activities and filled out a questionnaire detailing more than 600 aspects of how they felt about and managed time. The surveys were mainly conducted in January through March of 1986, with probability samples of adults in both cities; the city directory was the sample frame used in Jackson, while the election registers were the basis of the sample in Pskov.

The survey was remarkable, both in terms of the quantity and quality of data that were collected in this first joint Soviet-American survey. As in previous studies, respondents in Jackson gave information that was quite similar to that found in national studies. Moreover, data from Pskov seemed quite similar to those collected in other cities in the Soviet Union. Table 7.1 summarizes the background and methodology of the two studies, as described in more detail in Chapter 2.

Main Results

Our study has found that the daily schedules of men in the U.S. and USSR are more similar than those of American and Soviet women. That was mainly because most women in the Soviet Union under the age of 65 are employed. While 55 percent of women in Jackson were employed, some 80 percent of Pskov women were; the employment figures for men were 91 percent in Pskov and 85 percent in Jackson.

Employed women in Pskov also had longer workweeks (48 hours) than the employed women in Jackson (41 hours per week). Thus all women in Pskov averaged about 39 hours a week of work compared to about 23 hours a week for Jackson women. These figures included more than three hours a week commuting time in Pskov and less than two hours in Jackson.

Table 7.1
Comparative Summary of Survey Features

	U.S.	USSR
Survey city:	Jackson, Michigan	Pskov, Russian Republic
City size:	80,000	197,000
Number of Interviews:	710	2181
Survey Dates:	January-April 1986	January-February 1986
Age Composition	18-65	18-65
Interview Mode:	Personal; In-home Self-completion	Personal; In-home Self-completion
Information:	24-Hour diary 600+ Item questionnaire	24-Hour diary 600+ Item questionnaire
Selection Criteria:	City Directory+ Random selection in household	Voting Registration Lists+ Random selection in household

Despite their longer work hours, the Soviet women also spent about the same time in family care activities across the week. Soviet women spent more time preparing meals (which averaged about eight hours in the Soviet Union and 6 hours in the U.S.) and doing laundry (four hours in the Soviet Union and two hours in the U.S.). They also spent more time in child care (four hours in the Soviet Union and three hours in the U.S.), with an equivalent number of children as Jackson women in the survey. American women spent more time (seven hours per week) doing house cleaning than Pskov women (4.5 hours) and in plant and pet care; they also spent more time in non work-related travel (seven hours vs. five hours).

Women in Pskov spent more time sleeping and resting, U.S. women more time in grooming and eating at home. The end result was that Soviet women had about 11 hours less free time each week than American women. The American women used more of that free time in organizational activity (mainly at church services), watching television, in social life and conversation, and in sports and outdoor recreation. Soviet women, on the other hand, spent more free time reading, taking walks and relaxing.

On the other hand, the difference in work-related times of all men in Pskov (49 hours per week) and all Jackson men (41 hours per week) was much smaller. Some two hours of that difference was due to the longer commuting times in Pskov; that despite the fact that Jackson residents lived further away from their workplace than residents of Pskov, many of whom lived close enough to walk to work.

Soviet men did more household work related to food and meal preparation, American men more on cleaning the house. Soviet men did more child care, American men more in chauffeuring children and other family-related travel.

Like their female counterparts, Soviet men spent more time sleeping and resting, American men more time grooming and eating. As a result, American men had about four hours a week more free time than Soviet men. As was the case for women, U.S. men spent more time in organized religious activity, in watching TV and in social life. Soviet men spent more time reading, taking walks and attending movies and entertainment.

These results generally suggest a rather important difference in the locus of social life in the two countries. Soviet citizens appear to have more social contact at the workplace, including eating meals together. By the time the workday is done, there seems less need or opportunity for socializing outside of the immediate family.

Household Technology

Most Pskov families (85 percent) cooked with gas stoves, while in Jackson electric and gas stoves were about equally prevalent. Far higher proportions of Jackson households had microwave ovens than in Pskov. While refrigerators were almost universal in both cities, far higher proportions of Jackson households had food processors, dishwashers and coffee machines. In contrast, far more Pskov households had technology for canning and preserving food. The two sites were more similar in access to washing machines, vacuum cleaners and sewing machines. More Jackson households had bicycles (that adults ride) and both two-wheeled and four-wheeled motor vehicles.

With regard to communications access, far more households in Jackson had telephones, color TVs and stereo equipment. However, roughly equivalent proportions in the two cities had access to a television set (over 95 percent) and to a home library of more than 100 books (about 40 percent).

The two sites were also rather equivalent in access to home musical instruments. Americans had more pianos, more Soviets had accordions. About one in five respondents in both countries had access to a guitar. The same rough equivalence could be found for sports equipment in general. While slightly more Americans possessed collections of tools and cameras, more Soviets had access to checker or chess sets.

At the same time, our data make it clear that the two "superpowers" of the second half of the 20th century are surprisingly similar in several ecological, economic and sociological respects. Despite the differences noted above, and the many cultural and historical differences that separate us, the daily life of people in these two countries have had much in common—at least as far as the two cities we have the opportunity to observe to represent these countries.

We first found that there were many demographic similarities between the populations aged 18 to 65 in the cities of Pskov and Jackson. The age distribution was fairly similar and the ratio of men to women and of college educated to less educated were becoming more similar as well. Most adults remain married in the two communities, although there are many more unmarried residents of Jackson. Residents of Pskov, moreover, now have most of the modern amenities of urban living that Jackson residents enjoy, such as electricity, water and plumbing—as well as land for gardening. The availability of many household appliances in Pskov, such as refrigerators, stoves, washing machines, was becoming universal—as was the household technology that dominates free time, namely the television set.

Although higher proportions of Pskov men and women are employed than in Jackson, that situation has also become more similar across time—although for quite different reasons (early retirement in Pskov, more women working in Jackson). And although the structure of work time is more uniform in Pskov (in terms of weekend and shift work), most workers in the two cities work five days a week and during day shift hours. The distribution of occupation by skill level and by branch of the economy are also quite similar, as is the distribution of men and women working in these branches.

These similarities also extend to the ways of spending time in the two cities, as well as to how these time-use patterns are changing. By far the largest, and probably most significant historical shift, concerns the sexual distribution of household labor. Women in both Pskov and Jackson are doing less housework. The decline in housework seems to be tied to many outside factors, such as the availability of appliances, decreased numbers of children, or increases in the proportion of women working outside the home (particularly in Jackson). But the shift in the division of housework also appears to have arisen for reasons outside of this factor (e.g., because of attitudes, values, etc.).

Another main shift in time use also has come about in both countries due to the increased diffusion and sophistication of television over the past two decades. Television viewing time is up dramatically in both countries, and has been accompanied by decreases in television's main "functional equivalents," namely radio, movies and reading. The declines in these activities seem to be greater in the Soviet Union, but that may be due to the later stage of TV's diffusion in the USSR relative to the U.S. It also appears that certain educational activities in Pskov may have declined as a result of television.

Other changes in time use seem less noticeable or systematic than these two large shifts. By and large, work and personal care activities, as well as most free-time activities, seem basically unchanged from what they were twenty years ago.

The third area of similarity we have encountered in our joint project concerns the subjective variables of attitudes, expectations and estimations. Striking convergences have emerged both in the proportions of Pskov and Jackson respondents who say they are satisfied or involved in various activities and in the factors related to higher or lower satisfaction or involvement.

These areas of shared results in the matters of background, behavior and attitudes should not obscure some basic areas in which the citizens of the U.S. and the USSR clearly differ from one another. Pskov respondents were more likely to be in households with regular traditional family and work relationships: married, with children, working five days and no shifts. More Jackson respondents lived alone or in nuclear families, rather than in extended family units. Household technology was obviously more available and more sophisticated in Jackson households. Housing space was greater and distances to city and workplace much further in Jackson, as a result of the near universal availability of automobiles. The reverse of this is that Pskov residents had workplaces and many public facilities within walking distance of their homes.

Differences are also found in the daily activities in which people in the two cities engage. Pskov residents continue to spend more time working, mending clothes, waiting in lines, reading books, going to the movies and taking walks. Jackson respondents spend more time shopping, taking naps, eating in restaurants, attending church services, attending sports events, visiting friends, attending parties, watching television, reading newspapers and in non-work travel. Some of these cultural differences have narrowed over the years, most prominently television viewing, but all do continue to hold.

Finally we have found some fascinating, but still not well understood, differences in how Pskov and Jackson respondents reacted to the study's subjective questions. There are clear differences in how American and Soviet citizens responded to the satisfaction and happiness questions, both in the use of extreme scale categories and in the activities they enjoyed doing.

Work Attitudes

Soviet and American workers gave slightly contrasting answers to the survey's questions about work attitudes. On the one hand, higher proportions of American workers said they were involved in their work. On the other hand, a somewhat higher proportion of Soviet workers (58 percent) said they almost always worked to the full extent of their abilities than did American workers (44 percent).

The same type of contrast was found with regard to work attitudes. Higher proportions of Soviet workers said they were completely satisfied with their jobs overall and with the length of their workweeks; a higher proportion of American workers said they were just satisfied (i.e. more satisfied than not). At the same time, a higher proportion of American workers said they liked their jobs, and that they liked them very much.

Thus these responses can be seen as consistent with the observation that Soviet workers may have lower aspirations about work goals given greater standardization of work conditions. Soviet workers could be more satisfied because of the greater job security that goes with their positions.

Housework Activities and Attitudes

In general, more men in Jackson reported having some basic domestic housework skills than did men in Pskov. That was true for cooking, for laundry care, and for sewing and knitting. It was also true for gardening and repairing automobiles, not surprising given the lower automobile ownership rate in Pskov. With regard to other repair and carpentry skills, the proportions having skills were more equivalent between the two sites.

Routine domestic skills (cooking, laundry, etc.) were practically universal among women in Pskov and Jackson. More Jackson women reported being able to sew, more Pskov women reported the ability to knit and embroider. More Jackson women said they could repair appliances and automobiles, garden and do carpentry work, but more Pskov women say they could do house repair and do canning and preserving.

With regard to feelings about doing these tasks, the responses were much more similar in Pskov and Jackson. In both countries, taking care of children was by far the most positively valued domestic activity, and mending clothes the least liked. Soviet women also enjoyed knitting, gardening, sewing clothes, and preserving foods more than other housework activities, while the American women enjoyed gardening, preserving foods, clothes shopping and cooking. Soviet and American women also disliked repair activities more than other activities.

In contrast, men in both sites rated these repair activities as something they most liked to do (outside of child care); cooking and gardening were also enjoyed more than average. Sewing and knitting, along with mending and washing clothes were at the bottom of the men's list of favorite domestic activities in both countries.

Leisure Skills and Enjoyment

In general, Jackson residents rated their leisure skills higher than did residents of Pskov. That was particularly true for collecting, flower growing, photography, creative writing, playing billiards and cards, scientific hobbies, playing music and taking care of pets. The two areas of higher claimed skills among Soviet respondents were knitting/embroidering and playing chess.

The main areas of women's leisure skills were in dancing, flower growing and playing checkers/dominoes in both countries. Jackson women were more likely to rate playing cards and taking care of pets as leisure skill areas. Lowest skill areas for women in both countries were technical/scientific hobbies, creative writing, playing music, and taking care of pets.

For men, the highest skill areas in both countries were concentrated in playing checkers, cards and billiards. Skills in taking care of pets and photography were rated relatively higher by Jackson males and dancing and playing chess among Pskov men. Lowest areas for men in both sites were knitting, creative writing and playing music.

Movie theaters, stage theaters, museums, gymnasiums, swimming pools and restaurants were generally most highly rated places to spend free time. Hobby clubs and cafes/bars were rated relatively higher by

Soviet respondents, most particularly the circus. American women rated restaurants and indoor swimming activities relatively more favorably than did the Soviet women.

Directions for Future Research

Many of these differences and interpretations will become clarified after we have the time and opportunity over the next few years to delve more deeply into the sources of variation in these responses and aspects of life in the two societies.

Even though we now feel we have identified many of the most important differences in the two countries, our analyses have only scratched the surface. Differences in time use have only been examined for five factors—gender, employment status, age, education and marital status. We have only been able to examine these differences two factors at a time, rather than as part of a larger multivariate analysis or multiple regression.

We also have at our disposal more than 600 other pieces of information about each respondent in the survey, each of which has potential linkages to time use. They have linkages, as well, to each other and to the survey's background factors.

Our analyses thus far have also concentrated on one narrow aspect of time use—average durations per activity. Many such figures have limited meaning, because they lump together participants and non-participants. Thus, data on the work times of total populations are difficult to interpret when they include respondents who were not part of the paid labor force. In the same way, figures on average minutes per day going to the movies or participating in organizations obviously require elaboration in terms of number of participants involved and the average times spent per participant.

Much the same can be said for the other facets of activity recorded in the diaries. We have rich data on secondary activities, on the locations of activities and on social partners during activities that have not been examined at all. Data on the time of day of activities, or of locations for activity, are also available. Nor have we had the opportunity to examine how closely the pilot study data from Kerch and from the three Maryland cities match the results reported here.

Still, many of the previous unknown differences in the two country's styles of life have become clearer. How and why these two societies, with such radically different cultural values and forms of social organization, appear as similar as they do is a topic we look forward to investigating more closely in the years to come.

Notes

1. This last criterion was practically impossible to apply in the cities of the USSR, given the lack of statistics to identify suburban settlements. In also taking into account certain geographic, administrative, lifestyle and transportation factors, the 1965 plan defined the city by its formal administrative boundaries. We used the same definition in 1986, defining Pskov by its existing administrative and territorial boundaries.

2. *The Use of Time,* Ed. A. Szalai, et al. (1972) The Hague: Morton; *The Time Budget of the Urban Population,* Ed. B. T. Kolpakov and V. D. Patrushev, Moscow, 1971 {in Russian}. The American 1965–66 data were reported in J. Robinson, (1977), *How Americans Use Time: A Social-Psychological Analysis of Everyday Behavior.* New York: Praeger.

3. See, for example, *Tendencies for Change in Time Budget of Workers,* Moscow 1979; *Problems of the Study of Working and Non-Working Time, Moscow,* 1985 (in Russian).

4. "In the Liberated City," *Pskovskaia Pravda,* 1967, 10 August (in Russian).

5. "Pskov in 1985," *Pskovskaia Pravda,* 1986, 28 January.

6. "Pskov in 1985," op. cit.

7. "On the fulfillment of the state plan for the development of the economy of Pskov Oblast in 1965," *Pskovskaia Pravda,* 1966, 9 February.

Bibliography

1. American and West European

Allen, C. "Photographing the TV Audience." *Journal of Advertising Research, 8* (1) pp. 2–8, 1968.

Bechtel, R., C. Achelpohl, and Akers, R. "Correlates Between Observed Behavior and Questionnaire Responses in Television Viewing." In E.A. Rubenstein, G.A. Comstock, & J.P. Murray (eds.). *Television and Social Behavior. Reports and Papers, Vol. 4: Television in Day-to-Day Life: Patterns and Use.* Washington, D.C.: U.S. Government Printing Office, 1971.

Berk, R.A. and Berk, S.F. *Labor and Leisure at Home: Content and Organization of the Household Day.* Beverly Hills: Sage Publications, 1979.

Chapin, Stuart. Human Activity Patterns in the City: *Things People Do in Time and in Space.* New York: Wiley, 1974.

Coffin, Thomas. "Televisions Impact on Society." *American Psychologist, 10.* October, pp. 630–641, 1955.

Converse, P.E. "Country Differences in Time Use." In A. Szalai *Use of Time.* (ed), The Hague: Mouton, 1962.

DeGrazia, Sebastian. *Time, Work, and Leisure.* New York: Twentieth Century Fund, 1962.

Harvey, Andrew and Elliott, David *Time and Time Again.* Ottawa-Hull, Canada: Employment and Immigration Commission, 1986.

Hill, Daniel. "Implications of Home Production and Inventory Adjustment Processes for Time-of-Day Demand for Electricity" in F.P. Juster and Stafford (ed.). *Time, Goods, and Well-Being.* Ann Arbor, Michigan: Institute for Social Research, 1985.

Juster, F. Thomas. "The Validity and Quality of Time Use Estimates Obtained from Recall Diaries" in F.T. Juster & F.P. Stafford (eds.). *Time Goods, and Well-Being.* Ann Arbor, Michigan: Institute for Social Research, The University of Michigan, 1985.

Juster, F. Thomas and Stafford, Frank. *Time, Goods and Well-Being.* Ann Arbor, Michigan: Institute for Social Research, The University of Michigan, 1985.

Kish, Leslie. *Survey Sampling.* New York: Wiley, 1965.

Pleck, Joseph. *Working Wives and Husbands.* Beverly Hills: Sage Publications, 1985.

Robinson, John. "The Validity and Reliability of Diaries versus Alternative Time Use Measures" in F.T. Juster & F.T. Stafford (eds.). *Time, Goods and Well-Being.* Ann Arbor, Michigan: Institute for Social Research, The University of Michigan, pp. 43–62, 1985.

Robinson, John. "Television and Leisure Time A New Scenario." *Communication, 31.* 1, pp. 120–130, 1981.

Robinson, John. "Household Technology and Household Work." in S.F. Berk (ed.). *Women and Household Labor.* Beverly Hills: Sage Publications, pp. 257–277, 1980.

Robinson, John. *How Americans Use Time: A Social-Psychological Analysis of Everyday Behavior.* New York: Praeger, 1977.

Robinson, John. *Changes in American's Use of Time: 1965–1975,* Cleveland, Ohio: Communication Research Center, 1976.

Robinson, John; Converse, Philip and Szalai, Alexander. "Everyday Life in Twelve Countries." in A. Szalai (ed.). *The Use of Time.* The Hague, Netherlands: Mouton, pp. 113–144, 1972.

Robinson, John. "Television's Impact on Everyday Life: Some Cross-national Evidence" in Volume 4 of the U.S. Surgeon General's Committee: *Television and Social Behavior* (edited by Eli Rubenstein, George Comstock and John Murray). Washington, D.C.: Government Printing Office, pp. 410–431, 1972.

Szalai, Alexander et al. *The Use of Time.* The Hague, Netherlands: Mouton, 1972.

Szalai, Alexander; Ferge, Susan; Goguel, Claude; Patrushev, Vasily; Raymond, Henri; Scheuch, Erwin; and Schneider, Anncrose (1966). *The Multinational Comparative Time-Budget Research Project:* Report on the organization, methods, and experiences of the pilot study 1965–1966 and the preliminary results of 13 parallel time-budget surveys. Contributions to the Round Table on Time-Budgets at the VIIth World Congress of Sociology, Evian, September 1966. 68 p.; also published in: *American Behavioral Scientist.* Dec. 1966 *10* (4): 1–31 and under the title "Recherche comparative internationale sur les budgets-temps," in: *Etudes et Conjonctures.* Sept. 1966(9): pp. 103–188.

Vanek, Joann. "Time Spent in Housework." *Scientific American, 11.* pp. 116–120, 1974.

Walker, Kathryn. "Homemaking Still Takes Time" *Journal of Home Economics, 61.* October, pp. 621–624, 1969.

Zerubavel, Eviatar. *Hidden Rhythms: Schedules and Calendars in Social Life.* Chicago: University of Chicago Press, 1984.

2. Soviet Union (1970–1987)

Artemov, V. A. *Social Time: Problems of Study and Research* Novosibirsk: Nauka Publishers, 1987.

Artemov, V.A., Balykova, N.A., and Kalugina, Z.I. *The Time of the Urban Population: Planning and Use.* Novosibirsk, Nauka Publishers, Siberian Division, 1982.

Armetov, V.A. (ed.). *Survey of the Time Budgets of Residents of Cities and Villages.* Novosibirsk, 1981.

Armetov, V. A. (ed.). *Time in the City and the Conditions of Its Use.* Novosibirsk, 1976.

Basic Features of the Technique for Constructing and Calculating a Total Time Budget for the Population of an Economic Region. Novosibirsk, 1971.

Bogdanova, Z.A., Eliseeva, I.I., and Mosin, E.F. *Analysis of the Study of Time Budgets of Students in Higher Educational Institutions in 1969–1976.* Leningrad, 1983.

Bolgov, V.I. *The Time Budget Under Socialism.* Moscow, Nauka Publishers, 1973.

Bur'ian, T.I., and Korzheva, E.M. *Formalized Parameters of the Time Budgets of the Population.* Moscow, 1982.

Bur'ian, T.I., and Korzheva, E.M. *Forecasting of the Time Budget: Possibilities and Problems.* Moscow, 1981.

Dubson, B.I. *Socio-economic Problems of Free Time in Conditions of Conditions of Modern Capitalism.* Moscow, Nauka Publishers, 1980.

Free Time and Moral Upbringing. Moscow, Znanie Publishers, 1979.

Gordon, L.A., Klopov, E.V., and Onikov, A.A. *Features of the Socialist Way of Life: the Daily Life of Urban Workers Yesterday, Today and Tomorrow.* Moscow: Znanie Publishers, 1977.

Gordon, L., and Klopov, E. *Man After Work* (in English). Moscow, Nauka Publishers, 1972.

Gordon, L.A., and Rimashevskaia, I.M. *The Five-Day Work Week and Workers' Free Time.* Moscow. Mysl' Publishers, 1972.

Karpukhin, D., and Kuznitsova, N. *A Rational Time Budget for Workers and Problems of Achieving It.* Economic Sciences. Moscow, 1979.

Methodological Questions of the Study of Time Budgets. Novosibirsk, 1972.

Netsentko, A.V. *Socio-economic Problems of Free Time Under Socialism.* Leningrad, 1975.

Orlov, G.P. *Free Time as a Sociological Category.* Sverdlovsk, 1973.

Patrushev, V. D. *On the Study of Working and Non-Working Time.* Moscow, ISR, AS, USSR, 1985.

Patrushev, V. D. (ed.). *Problems of the Effectiveness of Measures on Improvement of the Use of the Population's Time Budget.* Moscow, ISR, AS, USSR, 1985.

Patrushev, V.D. *Time Budget of Industrial Workers* (Materials from the Study). Moscow, ISR, AS, USSR, 1984.

Patrushev, V.D. "Possible changes in the use of time budgets." *SI,* No. 1, 1982.

Patrushev, V.D. "Basic results and tasks of the study of time budgets in the USSR." *SI,* No. 7, 1981

Patrushev, V.D., Tatarova, G.G., and Tolstova, U.N. "Multidimensional typology of time-expenditure." *SI,* No. 1, 1980

Patrushev, V.D. (ed.). *Indices of Time in Socio-economic Planning.* Moscow, ISR, AS, USSR, 1981.

Patrushev, V.D. "Satisfaction with free time as a social indicator," *SI,* No. 1, 1979.

Patrushev, V.D. (ed.). *Tendencies for Change in the Time Budget of Workers.* Moscow, ISR, AS, USSR, 1979.

Patrushev, V.D. *The Use of the Total Time of Society (Problems of the Time Budgets of the Population.* Moscow, Mysl' Publishers, 1978.

Patrushev, V.D. *Time Budget of the Rural Population.* Moscow, 1977.

Patrushev, V.D. *Problems of the Activity of Workers Outside of Production.* Moscow, ISR, AS, USSR, 1976.

Patrushev, V.D. "Distribution of the total fund of time of the population its significance for socio-economic planning." *SI,* No. 1, 1975.

Patrushev, V.D. "General regularities and features in the use of time-budget of the employed urban population in socialist and capitalist countries." *Society and Leisure,* N1. pp. 99–122, 1974.

Patrushev, V.D., Kutyrev, B., and Podovalova, R. "Tendencies and changes in the mass of working time and possibilities of curtailing it," *SI,* No. 1, 1973.

Patrushev, V.D., and B.T. Kolpakov, *Budget of the Urban Population.* Moscow, Statistika Publishers, 1971.

Patrushev, V.D., and Podovalova, R. "Working time: use and reserves," No. 6, 1970.

Pimenova, V.N. *Free Time in Socialist Society.* Moscow, Nauka Publishers, 1974.

Prudenskii, G.A. *Problems of the Study of Working and Non-Working Time.* Moscow, Nauka Publishers, 1972.

Questions of Methodology and Technique of the Time Budget Study. Collection of articles in two books. Moscow, ISR, AS, USSR, 1980.

Questions of the Use and Forecasting of Time Budgets. Novosibirsk, 1973.

Suprun, P. T. *The Time Budget of Workers.* Moscow, Ekonomika Publishers, 1972.

Time Indices in Socio-Economic Planning of a City. Novosibirsk, 1977.

The Time Budget of the Residents of Pskov. *(Materials of the International Study of Time Budgets.)* Novosibirsk, 1973.

Zaikina, G.A. *The Structure of the Free Time of the Population of Lenkoran' Socio-professional and Age Differentiation,* 1981.

Zborovskii, M. M. *The Work Day, Its Structure and Use.* Kiev, 1970.

INDEX